Building Bridges:
Collaboration Within and Beyond the Academic Library

CHANDOS
INFORMATION PROFESSIONAL SERIES

Series Editor: Ruth Rikowski
(email: Rikowskigr@aol.com)

Chandos' new series of books are aimed at the busy information professional. They have been specially commissioned to provide the reader with an authoritative view of current thinking. They are designed to provide easy-to-read and (most importantly) practical coverage of topics that are of interest to librarians and other information professionals. If you would like a full listing of current and forthcoming titles, please visit our web site **www.chandospublishing.com** or contact Hannah Grace-Williams on email info@chandospublishing.com or telephone number +44 (0) 1865 884447.

New authors: we are always pleased to receive ideas for new titles; if you would like to write a book for Chandos, please contact Dr Glyn Jones on email gjones@chandospublishing.com or telephone number +44 (0) 1865 884447.

Bulk orders: some organisations buy a number of copies of our books. If you are interested in doing this, we would be pleased to discuss a discount. Please contact Hannah Grace-Williams on email info@chandospublishing.com or telephone number +44 (0) 1865 884447.

Building Bridges: Collaboration Within and Beyond the Academic Library

ANNE LANGLEY
EDWARD G. GRAY
AND
K.T.L. VAUGHAN

Chandos Publishing
Oxford · England

Chandos Publishing (Oxford) Limited
Chandos House
5 & 6 Steadys Lane
Stanton Harcourt
Oxford OX29 5RL
UK
Tel: +44 (0) 1865 884447 Fax: +44 (0) 1865 884448
Email: info@chandospublishing.com
www.chandospublishing.com

First published in Great Britain in 2006

ISBN:
1 84334 151 4 (paperback)
1 84334 200 6 (hardback)

British Library Cataloguing-in-Publication Data.
A catalogue record for this book is available from the British Library.

Typeset by Domex e-Data Pvt. Ltd.
Printed in the UK and USA.

Printed in the UK by 4edge Limited - www.4edge.co.uk

Contents

Acknowledgements

The authors would like to thank all of their colleagues, and the many librarians and university faculty and staff who gave us ideas and stories for this book. Without their insight and enthusiastic conversations, this book would not have come into being.

Preface

To introduce something altogether new would mean to begin all over, to become ignorant again, and to run the old, old risk of failing to learn. (Isaac Asimov)

For many librarians, collaboration can seem a risky venture. Collaborative projects often require that we work with people whose work styles, responsibilities, and culture are very different from our own. We think if we enter into collaborations we will probably have to go above and beyond our regular responsibilities. We also recognise that before starting out we probably only have a rudimentary understanding of the types of work that collaboration may require. Collaboration can take us outside of our comfort zone.

However, once we step back and take a broader view of the work that we as librarians do, then collaboration looks to be a given – a natural way of operating. If we start from the premise that we, as academic library staff, are primarily in the business of connecting people with information, then we can take our thinking one step further to the idea that thinking and working collaboratively is inherent to that connection. The work we do, in and of itself, involves a huge variety of tasks: finding, buying, organising, making accessible, monitoring, preserving, and housing information. And for anyone doing any of these tasks, we intimately know that there is a lot of overlap among them. In addition, for most of these areas of work, there is a part of each that involves interacting with other people, be they librarians, paraprofessionals, patrons or library users, faculty, vendors, who knows? The opportunities for interacting are limitless. These opportunities are where collaboration comes into play.

> Opportunities are usually disguised as hard work, so most people don't recognize them. (Ann Landers)

Collaborations bring like-minded people together to work towards shared goals. The information explosion has increased the rate of change in higher education, as well as in the workplace, and in our everyday lives. In turn the number of shared goals across formal and informal work boundaries have also increased. Through collaborations we can sometimes decrease everyone's workload, because we are not reinventing the wheel, or working at cross-purposes. So while collaboration may seem risky, not to collaborate can be even riskier.

> Great discoveries and improvements invariably involve the cooperation of many minds. (Alexander Graham Bell)

Collaboration is necessary. Organisations, departments and individuals that refuse to, or who are unable to collaborate, will find themselves pushed farther out to the margins. They will face unnecessary roadblocks to getting work done because they don't communicate or collaborate with those who share the same goals, or whose work overlaps with their own. Money, time and effort will be wasted. In the most extreme instances, resentment will arise because those who ought to have collaborated didn't. They went out on their own, did it without any input or ideas from outside, and now the work they did is incompatible with the work of those who are the recipients of it. Sounds extreme, but as we look into the crystal ball of the future, we predict that library staff have got to start collaborating, and doing it well, or they may very well find themselves without jobs in the field of academic information access and provision. To remain relevant, collaboration is key.

Our goal with this book is to help you, whether you want to get started as a collaborator if you aren't one yet, or if you just want to hone your collaboration skills. We provide tools and guidelines for collaborating for those who need them, and offer ideas on where to start. The case studies cover real collaborations, although we have changed the names and other details for confidentiality. The studies are grouped together to be useful for planning or they can be used to generate ideas for projects of your own.

> The most important function of education at any level is to develop the personality of the individual and the significance of his life to himself and to others. This is the basic architecture of a life; the rest is ornamentation and decoration of the structure. (Grayson Kirk)

In the writing of this book we culled from our own experiences, conducted interviews with library staff from a variety of academic institutions, and undertook a thorough review of the literature. We recognise that there are many ways to collaborate, and that the scale of a project varies with each new collaborative undertaking. For example, when planning for the design and outfitting of an instruction room in a library, it will be necessary for various departments to collaborate: instruction librarians, systems or technology support staff, and in-house trainers will all need to work together closely in considering room layout, determining hardware and software needs, choosing appropriate furniture, taking into account all access and security issues, and even considering budgetary concerns. This will probably be a very short-term collaboration. Longer collaborations may last for extended periods of time – curriculum-based library instruction between librarians and professors may last multiple semesters, while consortia can continue collaborating for years. However, whether short or long term, we propose that all collaborations have similarities.

Collaboration, as we define it for this book, may only comprise a small part of a project, or the entire project may be a collaboration. We recognise that you will not use all the tips, techniques and tools in this book for every project. We have, therefore, made a concerted effort to organise the contents so that you can pick and choose sections to read as you need. You are welcome to read the book cover to cover, and then come back to it at your leisure for a reference or reminder. If you do read it in its entirety, our intent is that it will give you a thorough overview of collaboration as it is practised in academic libraries today.

In the broadest sense of the word, many of us are already collaborating in some way at work. Yet, while we are collaborating, we must continually ask ourselves, are we and our libraries getting the most out of the collaborations? We think the answer is probably not. So, we invite you and your libraries to challenge yourselves to get more out of your collaborations by improving your skills as individual collaborators.

> You know ... that a blank wall is an appalling thing to look at. The wall of a museum – a canvas – a piece of film – or a guy sitting in front of a typewriter. Then,

you start out to do something – that vague thing called creation. The beginning strikes awe within you. (Edward Steichen)

All three of us have found that collaborations are a way to share the work, learn new things, be more accountable, and more productive. We are here to tell you that all of our collaborative projects have led to other collaborative projects in turn. Be prepared to grow personally and professionally once you begin collaborating – it can't be helped!

About the authors

Anne Langley has worked in academic libraries since 1987 and has been a professional librarian since 1993. Having been employed in four academic libraries and the library of a large national research laboratory, she is now Associate Librarian at Duke University, and Adjunct Associate Professor for the Duke University Department of Chemistry. Anne holds a BA in Creative Writing from Georgia State University, and an MLIS from the University of Tennessee, Knoxville. She has held positions in almost all areas of the academic library: technical services, collections services, public services, administration, management, and on various digital projects. Her publications and presentations cover research and projects in all areas of academic librarianship.

Edward Gray is the Public Services Librarian for the Biological and Environmental Sciences Library at Duke University. He received his BS in Geography from Louisiana State University and then went on to receive his MS in Geography and MLIS from the University of Tennessee. His research interests include public services in science libraries, citation analysis of biological literature, and collection development.

K.T.L. Vaughan is the Librarian for Bioinformatics and Pharmacy at the University of North Carolina at Chapel Hill Health Sciences Library and Clinical Assistant Professor of

Pharmaceutical Education in the UNC School of Pharmacy. She has also held positions in two other ARL institutions and a US Environmental Protection Agency library. She holds an AB in Biology from Harvard University and an MSLS from UNC-CH. Her research interests include the information habits of scientists and clinicians, the librarian's role in bioinformatics research, and the recruitment, retention, and development of science librarians.

The authors may be contacted via the publishers.

Why collaborate?

Most successful men have not achieved their distinction by having some new talent or opportunity presented to them. They have developed the opportunity that was at hand. (Bruce Marton)

Introduction

This chapter details all the reasons you would want or need to collaborate. If you are having trouble figuring out whether the project you want to do can be done collaboratively, or if you want to collaborate with others but your boss, supervisor, colleagues, or home institution need(s) convincing, this chapter will provide you with an extensive list of reasons why collaboration will work for you. These reasons can also serve as a planning checklist when doing your initial project planning. By going through the sections one by one and describing your project as it fits into each part, you will have a clearer picture of why you are collaborating. This activity can make the collaboration process more efficient and focused. It will be easier to stay on track with the project and your individual tasks even when you are up to your elbows in the dirty dishwater of everyday work.

Background

I am convinced that the future progress of chemistry as an exact science depends very much upon the alliance with mathematics. (A. Frankland)

We always find that it is good to start with a definition. It gets everyone on the same page, and then we all have a common ground to begin our discussion.

Adapted from *Merriam-Webster's Collegiate Dictionary*:

Collaborate
  Main Entry: col·lab·o·rate
  Pronunciation: kə-la'-bə-'rāt
  Function: intransitive verb
  Inflected Form(s): -rat·ed; -rat·ing
  Etymology: Late Latin *collaboratus*, past participle of *collaborare* to labour together, from Latin *com-* + *laborare* to labour; more at **LABOUR**
  Date: 1871
  1. to work jointly with others or together especially in an intellectual endeavour
  2. to cooperate with or willingly assist an enemy of one's country and especially an occupying force
  3. to cooperate with an agency or instrumentality with which one is not immediately connected

Cooperate
  Main Entry: co·op·er·ate
  Pronunciation: kō'ä-pə-'rāt
  Function: intransitive verb
  Etymology: Late Latin *cooperatus*, past participle of *cooperari*, from Latin *co-* + *operari* to work; more at **OPERATE**

Date: 1582
1. to act or work with another or others: act together or in compliance <refused to *cooperate* with the police>
2. to associate with another or others for mutual benefit <nations *cooperating* in a trade agreement>

Semantics can often get in the way of a group of people having a common understanding of their shared purpose. Experience suggests that many people often have in mind the definition of a word based on context, rather than a literal definition. These context-derived definitions can get us into trouble when we start working together, as meaning can be altered or shaded by individual experiences and personalities. So, as we do above, you may also want to do in your collaborative work – clarify and agree on the literal meanings of the words you use with each other. The earlier in the process that you do this the better.

Now that we not only have a common, literal definition of 'collaborate', but also its sister verb 'cooperate', we can embark on why collaboration is a useful, efficient work tool.

> If you never ask yourself any questions about the meaning of a passage, you cannot expect the book to give you any insight you do not already possess. (Mortimer J. Adler)

Solve a common problem

About ten years ago in a library strategic planning meeting we were talking about how it was becoming ever more important that different library departments learn what the others were doing. We realised that in this increasingly complex environment, actions, work, and decisions that were being made in one department had a major impact on other departments, in ways that they never had before. More people needed to be consulted before policy decisions were made; workflow decisions had to involve all departments and staff who did the work needed to be included in the discussion. This was necessary to make sure that handing over of work from one department to another occurred where the work was in a format usable to those who were receiving the information. As technology became entrenched in every part of the work of the library, these types of problems grew in number and size.

We began to solve these problems using decision-trees. Then came teams and quality circle management, where the staff that do the work help to make the decisions affecting the work. We quickly found that staff involvement needed to occur even earlier in the process. Those working across departments needed to talk directly to one another, instead of having only their managers communicating. So committees, matrices, and task forces were formed and comprised of the people who were doing the work, no matter what department they came from: reference, technical services, collection development, circulation, systems, etc.

These types of collaborative working environments have now expanded to include people from not only all library departments, but also, when appropriate, university administrators, faculty, students, and colleagues from similar libraries, locally as well as those further away. Now, for example, we have curriculum-based library instruction (faculty/librarian collaboration) and consortial collection management activities (librarian/librarian/administrative collaboration). Our work environments can and do extend far beyond the walls of the library.

Librarians have always understood the need to work cooperatively and collaboratively. For example, the authors' local library consortium, Triangle Research Libraries Network (TRLN) was started in 1979 and has a long history of collaboration. At a keynote address to the University of North Carolina-Chapel Hill (UNC-CH) Librarians' Association on 14 March 2005, Dr Jose Marie Griffiths, Dean of the UNC-CH School of Information and Library Science, discussed the serious need for librarians to collaborate with each other and with our stakeholders. This need for collaboration will only increase as librarians' roles in this new technologically enhanced information retrieval world change and involve more user-instigated activities. In order to find our appropriate place in the new provision and organisation of information, we have to work hand-in-hand, or collaborate if you will, with each other and our stakeholders.

> We cannot live for ourselves alone. Our lives are connected by a thousand invisible threads, and along these sympathetic fibers, our actions run as causes and return to us as results. (Herman Melville)

Common problems, common needs

So why this book? Historically, collaboration took place at higher administrative levels of the academic library, while those on the front lines of library work – the reference librarians, the cataloguers, and the support staff – were often the only beneficiaries of the collaborative work of their managers and library administrators. Now the need to collaborate has expanded to include library workers at all levels of the library. Not only do we need to collaborate across departmental boundaries, we need to collaborate with those outside of the library.

Not all of us are prepared to collaborate. Some of us don't have the skills necessary to successfully collaborate across unfamiliar boundaries that exist not only inside of our own library walls, but also beyond them. Nor do we all have a frame of reference of what expectations may be in collaborative projects or collaborative work tasks.

While in collaborative projects we often have common needs. It can be a major hurdle for the project's participants when different people and different departments have different styles of approaching work and of getting work done. For example, public service librarians operate on a yearly schedule that responds to the semesters or terms of the students in the institution where they work. On the other hand, technical services librarians commonly work on an annual financial calendar, imposed by their institution. And finally, faculty commonly work on a term or semester-based calendar for their teaching responsibilities, but often spend their summers doing research and/or teaching. These schedules rarely coincide and can wreak havoc when people on different schedules are planning collaborative projects.

> Our lives improve only when we take chances – and the first and most difficult risk we can take is to be honest with ourselves. (Walter Anderson)

This book aims to provide a framework for collaboration no matter what part of the library you work in. As such, these obstacles are highlighted so that you can recognise that they will affect how you design your project. In no way do we intend to discourage anyone from undertaking collaborative projects. Collaboration is often the only way we can get work done!

Patience and perseverance have a magical effect before which difficulties disappear and obstacles vanish. (John Quincy Adams)

Different skill sets to solve a problem

As we have already seen, so much of the work in planning collaborative projects involves figuring out how the work will get done and then how it will travel across formal boundaries. Now we will focus on the skills needed to do the project work itself. Because collaborations cross formal work boundaries, we must often bring people together who have wildly different skill sets. Many collaborative ventures will require all of these various skill sets for the project to succeed. When thinking about a collaboration participant's skills, it is useful to remember that some individual skill sets are an outcome of the type of work we do, and others are part of our own personal working style.

Certain defects are necessary for the existence of individuality. (Johann Wolfgang von Goethe)

For example, technical services librarians are often very detail-oriented and able to focus for extended periods of time on problems of immense complexity. Faculty know how to navigate the university bureaucracy for scheduling classes, assigning grades, and reserving rooms. They also have in-depth knowledge of the curriculum of their field, and classroom teaching experience. In addition, they can share their own information research styles during a library instruction session. Conversely, instruction librarians are well-versed on teaching information literacy, they know what can (or cannot) fit into a single class period, and they are experts in search techniques and navigating through the universe of information resources.

When planning your project, keep in mind the strengths and skills of the various participants. While playing to people's strengths is always a good idea, be open to those participants who are enthusiastic about learning a new skill or may want to try something they have never had the opportunity to do. Getting the work done is important, but growing as individuals and increasing our skills are very important parts of collaboration.

> Learning is not attained by chance, it must be sought for with ardor and diligence. (Abigail Adams)

Increase supporting resources

This reason to collaborate seems rather obvious; however, you will probably want to remind objectors to your project of this powerful incentive to collaborate. When you collaborate with people from other departments and institutions, the costs and resources that are used can be shared by all members of the project. You and those working with you can bring work skills, time, computer time, office supplies, classroom space, or whatever the project requires to the tasks of the collaboration. You then increase the resources that can be collectively applied to the project. In concert, the burden lies with all partners, not just with one department or institution.

> Scientists tend to resist interdisciplinary inquiries into their own territory. In many instances, such parochialism is founded on the fear that intrusion from

other disciplines would compete unfairly for limited financial resources and thus diminish their own opportunity for research. (Hannes Alfven)

Build communities

Collaboration is a win-win adventure where the process of collaborating is quite possibly more important than the end product that we are working towards. Through collaborative projects, we increase the number of people with whom we can work on future projects. Once we work with these people, we have collectively built upon our now shared knowledge and experience. As we will see in some of the case studies, many first-time collaborative ventures grow and change into more and often different collaborative ventures from those worked on at the outset. Once you have begun collaborating, you find that you will have created a team of collaborators who now have the skills, who know the needs and quite possibly also know the long-term goals, of each of the partners. New collaborations can then take place quite easily with that shared knowledge and increased skill.

> Small opportunities are often the beginning of great enterprises. (Demosthenes)

Respond to cross-boundary needs

One of the most powerful effects of the technological age on the workplace is that people from various departments and institutions must now work closely together to get work done. Boundaries are blurred and goals are often shared.

This means that we now have to work with, and do work for, people whose work-flow, habits, and ethics are often very different from our own. This requires us to be more collaborative in the way we work. For example, no longer can a library systems department make the best decisions about what software to make available on the computers in a training room. It takes the system department's knowledge about available hardware and software, and instruction librarians' knowledge of the logistics of teaching with computers, to create a workable instruction space that can by used by the instruction librarians and supported by the systems department. Without the collaborative input from staff in both areas of the library, the instruction space would most likely be difficult to use and/or hard to maintain. It takes the unique knowledge from both departments to create a space that will work for everyone.

> Whatever affects one directly, affects all indirectly. I can never be what I ought to be until you are what you ought to be. This is the interrelated structure of reality. (Martin Luther King, Jr.)

Respond to shared goals

Intentionally or not, different departments and institutions will have often shared goals. To attain these shared goals, everyone's involvement is necessary. Because the library wants to make materials accessible to users, this requires the work and thoughts of staff from both technical and public services. No one department can make the decisions or carry out the work alone; they must collaborate. For example, hiring a librarian to manage the electronic resources purchasing and continuous access issues is a task where reference librarians, acquisitions librarians, cataloguing librarians, and the web development librarians will all have a vested interest in how the job gets done. Thus, a search committee would need to represent all these differing constituents in some way during the job design and hiring process. They would need to collaborate closely with one another, and make sure that whoever they hire has good collaboration skills.

> There is more similarity in the marketing challenge of selling a precious painting by Degas and a frosted mug of root beer than you ever thought possible. (A. Alfred Taubman)

Operate outside of a formal structure

While we need formal structures in bureaucracies, they are often a hindrance in getting work done quickly and efficiently. When staff from two or three discrete departments are trying to work together, there is not likely to be an existing formal structure for working together, and so they will need to create their own structure. The creation of a new structure can be a major part of any collaboration. It is important to define the structures – both formal and informal – early on in the process, for each participant's home department or institution. Because you must decide how you will work together and who will get the work done, discussing work structures early in the process will ensure you figure out how to fit in with the structures of each of the participants. Collaboration often takes place outside of any formal structure. In a collaborative venture, the participants can and need to decide on the structure of their governance without relying on any formal structure.

People tend to work in teams, in a collaborative way, in an informal network. If you create an environment like that, it's much more effective and much more efficient. (Jim Mitchell)

As we have mentioned numerous times above, more and more of the work we do demands that we work collaboratively, not only to get things done, but to get them done effectively. There are so many new areas in our work where the types of work we will be doing are not yet defined. Getting a new information system for the library, creating an instructional vision for the library where previously it was individually driven, developing curriculum-based library instruction classes, or even just getting university students the help they need to find the resources for a particular class assignment – all of these situations are areas for probable collaboration in the library and beyond. A new information system will mean changed workflows, new and possibly overlapping responsibilities, and definitely no more business as usual. So much has changed, so much is changing, and so much will change that collaboration is the only way we will be able to respond to these changes effectively.

Personal gains

Many of us like to work with others. We often do our best work by not going it alone. When working with others, we find we can be more creative and more productive, with less procrastination, all while creating higher-quality products. We have to acknowledge that no single person is terrific at everything. By working together, we can be more thorough and more productive as we play to our strengths by doing what we are good at, leaving what we aren't good at to those with the necessary skills. We can also increase our skills by working with people with different skills. We can learn from them, or at least, learn to appreciate other ways of working.

> Keep things informal. Talking is the natural way to do business. Writing is great for keeping records and putting down details, but talk generates ideas. Great things come from out luncheon meetings which consist of a sandwich, a cup of soup, and a good idea or two. No martinis. (T. Boone Pickens)

Obvious areas for collaboration

To get you thinking about possible areas to begin collaborative projects, we have provided the following list:

1. As it is a waste of time to do bibliographic instruction without integration into curricula, it is virtually impossible to offer it without collaborating in some way with the instructor/professor.

2. When deciding to purchase multidisciplinary databases, how do all the parties affected make a joint decision that you will all support and can all live with? On a very small scale this is collaboration.

3. There are still no standards for handling digital information – the boundaries are blurred and there is no more black and white in what and how to access. Public services and technical services librarians must work together.

4. Get help and ideas from colleagues who are similar: geographically, subject area or type of librarian, related

faculty, people with similar interests and/or needs, new projects with no standard way of doing business.

Further reading

Armstrong, K. (2004) 'The shared bibliographer: TRLN builds cooperative South Asia Collection'. *Against the Grain* 16(3): 24.

Backhus, S. H. and Summey, T. P. (2003) 'Collaboration: the key to unlocking the dilemma of distance reference services'. *The Reference Librarian* 83/84: 193–202.

Berry, T. U. Shrode, F. G. (2003) 'Cooperative reference and collection development: the science and technology group at the university of Tennessee libraries'. *The Reference Librarian* 83/84: 145–55.

Buxton, K. A. and Gover, H. R. (2003) 'A national laboratory and university branch campus library partnership: shared benefits and challenges from combined reference services'. *The Reference Librarian* 83/84: 251–62.

D'Angelo, B. J. (2003) 'If they build it will they come? Cooperation and collaboration to create a customized library'. *The Reference Librarian* 83/84: 237–50.

Dickson, V. (2004) 'Collaboration plus! The development of an information literacy and communication program'. *Australian Library Journal* 53(2): 153–60.

Guard, R. (2005) 'Musings on collaboration and vested interest'. *The Journal of Academic Librarianship* 31(2): 89–91

Hardesty, L. (2004) 'Successful partnering to transform the college library: an interview with Richard Ekman'. *Portal* 4(4): 455–63

Kreitz, P. A. (2004) 'Librarians as knowledge builders: Strategic partnering for service and advocacy'. *College & Research Libraries News* 65(1): 8–10, 15.

Markgraf, J. S. (2003) 'Collaboration between distance education faculty and the library: one size does not fit all'. *Journal of Library Administration* 37(3/4): 451–64.

Naslund, J.-A., Asselin, M. and Filipenko, M. (2005) 'Blueprint for collaboration: an information literacy project at the University of British Columbia' *PNLA Quarterly* 69(3): 10, 29–32.

O'Connor, S. (2004) 'Collaborative strategies for low-use research materials'. *Library Collections, Acquisitions, and Technical Services*, 28(1): 51–7.

Riedel, T. (2003) 'Added value, multiple choices: librarian/faculty collaboration in online course development'. *Journal of Library Administration* 37(3/4): 477–87.

Stamatoplos, A. and Mackoy, R. (2004) 'Collaboration in library research'. *Indiana Libraries* 23(1): 2–5.

Tucker, J. C., Bullian, J. and Torrence, M. C. (2003) 'Collaborate or die! Collection development in today's academic library'. *The Reference Librarian* 83/84: 219–36.

2

Building foundations for collaboration

Introduction

Some organisations and departments are already fertile environments for collaboration. Projects sprout up like seedlings in a garden and are carefully tended so that they can grow and mature. The staff are ready, prepared, and well-supported by their organisation so that they can easily enter into collaborative projects. Other organisations and departments are organised in such a way where initiating collaborative projects and then working on them would be very foreign to the way they normally work. In organisations where collaboration is not supported or understood, staff proposing collaborative projects can find their suggestions falling on deaf ears.

We are in a time of rapid technological change and are witnessing increasing interdisciplinarity of all aspects of our work. Consequently, many library and information science leaders are discovering that the need for collaboration is increasing. The updated norm for success is that most, if not all of us, will have to collaborate with both internal and external partners in order to get our work done. While this may be a new way of approaching work for many, for a few people, it is old hat.

The big question for this chapter is not *should* we collaborate, or *can* we collaborate, but how can we make sure our environment supports collaboration? Furthermore, do we and our colleagues have the skills and attributes of good collaborators? More specifically, what are these collaboration skills and attributes? We may need to learn new ways of working, alone and together, as well as learning how to incorporate all the possible different ways of communicating and sharing work with one another. Many of these communication types can be very different from what we are accustomed.

Finally, what can you do if your workplace does not support collaboration, and you find yourself in the tight spot of mutually needing something done, but one or more of your partners does not have the support of their department/library/institution? This situation was encountered by one of the library directors we interviewed. His local state legislature was not interested in supporting a state-wide project between selected public libraries and state and private college libraries. The library directors independently decided that collaboration was necessary to solve their problems, and together they decided to progress without the support of the state government.

The collaborators met, planned out the project, went back to their home institutions, got the work done, and wound up with the results they were looking for. Their covert actions paid off and formed the basis for a state-wide library consortium that still exists today. This consortium has grown, become a more formal entity, gained new partners, and as you can imagine from their evident successes, now has the blessing and support of the state government. Don't underestimate the power of need and how having a common purpose can inspire people to work together. Almost nothing is more powerful.

Nothing in this world can take the place of persistence. Talent will not; nothing is more common than unsuccessful people with talent. Genius will not; unrewarded genius is almost a proverb. Education will not; the world is full of educated derelicts. Persistence and determination alone are omnipotent. The slogan 'press on' has solved and always will solve the problems of the human race. (Calvin Coolidge)

Personal attributes

Collaborations are made up of individuals. Each individual brings their own attributes: skill, knowledge and talent, to the collective collaborative effort. The success or failure of any collaboration depends on the combined skills, knowledge and talents of its members. Below are descriptions of the personal attributes which, if present in the collaborative partners, will ensure that the project will successful. As you, and only you, are in control of yourself and your personal attributes, now is the time to cultivate them if you want to begin or improve upon your collaborating.

Flexibility

I am a man of fixed and unbending principles, the first of which is to be flexible at all times. (Everett Dirkson)

Originally when we were planning the structure of this chapter we put the section on flexibility somewhere in the middle. However, after our meetings and discussions with collaborators of all kinds, we found they all agreed and emphasised that flexibility was the single most vital attribute of successful collaborations. Without flexibility, collaboration falls flat. So, while all the other skills discussed in this chapter are important for collaboration, without flexibility you will not be a good collaborator. So if you want to be a good collaborator, but are not yet flexible, commit yourself now to improving your flexibility.

Before we go into an in-depth discussion of flexibility, let's consider what do you do when, as an individual, you are willing and able to collaborate, but the organisation or department where you work is not. You have some options, a few involving risk, and others involving inaction. You will have to decide how important this particular venture is to you and the work you want get done.

In the event you have to proceed without the support of your department/institution etc., we offer these somewhat risky options to help you decide what to do:

- Enter into the collaboration without the knowledge, support, etc. of your organisation, preferably starting with a smaller pilot project. If this smaller project is successful, when you share your project's success with your organisation, you can report that you tried it out as a pilot project and present the results accordingly. With this method, you can perhaps gain the support you need to continue with the full-scale project. If the pilot project wasn't successful, however, you may have to go back to the drawing board and figure out why, and try again. If you think it failed *because* you didn't have the support of your organisation, then you will have to think about how to sell it, if indeed you and your collaborative partners really want to continue.

- Enlist the support of your collaborative partners and their organisation to help sell it to your organisation. Warning: This could backfire and alienate you from your home organisation. Only you can decide if the project is worth that risk. Polish up your influencing skills and powers of persuasion, then combine them with an extensive collaboration plan so as to lend your project the heft and girth it needs to be accepted. You may also want to look for possible tie-ins with your organisation's mission and vision statements.

> There are a lot of great technicians in advertising. And unfortunately they talk the best game. They know all the rules ... but there's one little rub. They forget that advertising is persuasion, and persuasion is not a science, but an art. Advertising is the art of persuasion. (William Bernbach)

Less risky options include:

- doing nothing;
- initiating discussions at your organisation about your project in particular, and/or collaboration in general. Get a conversation started about collaboration as a viable problem-solving option. Then perhaps you could suggest your project as a test.

So what are the attributes of flexibility? Once again we turn to a literal definition of the word to make sure that we all have the same context.

Adapted from *Merriam-Webster's Collegiate Dictionary*:

Flexible
Main Entry: **flex·i·ble**
Pronunciation: 'flek-s&-b&l
Function: adjective
Date: fifteenth century

1. capable of being flexed: pliant
2. yielding to influence: tractable
3. characterised by a ready capability to adapt to new, different, or changing requirements *syn* see **ELASTIC**

In collaborative situations the third definition is the one we use in this book: 'a ready capability to adapt to new, different, or changing requirements'. So what does this mean in a practical sense?

Let's break this definition down into some manageable and discrete parts. First 'characterised by a ready capability'. This reminds us of the phrase, 'ready, willing and able'. Specifically, you are able to start work right away, you have the desire to do so, and you have the skills and experience necessary to begin working.

Second, 'to adapt', or can you change direction at the drop of a hat, or are you at least willing to try? Are you one of those people who can take a few minutes out of every day and consider whether or not the way you are currently working is the best, most efficient, workable way to approach the work problem in front of you? And if you decide that the answer is no, do you find out what will work better, and then change how you do the work?

Third, 'new, different, or changing requirements' – sounds like a collaboration in the making. Often when you collaborate, most of what you are doing will be new, and as it *is* new, it will be different from much of what you have done before. As with practically all of our work now, what you do and how you do it will constantly change. Not entirely, and not all at once. But in small, medium and sometimes major ways, work will be changing constantly. Go back to 'to adapt' above and once you incorporate adaptability into your way of working, you will be able to handle this constant change. It becomes a positive helix, gaining speed and capability as it spirals upward.

Strong networking skills

> It's all about people. It's about networking and being nice to people and not burning any bridges. Your book is going to impress, but in the end it is people that are going to hire you. (Mike Davidson)

Do you talk to strangers? Do you go up and introduce yourself to people you don't know but who you suspect may have similar needs or interests as your own? Do you make connections between people and their strengths and interests and then tell those people about those connections? Do you do favours for others and know how to call in favours fairly? Do you keep in reasonable contact with colleagues, contacts, others and not just when you need them, but when you find something that may interest them?

Networking is a learned skill. Collaboration, for the most part, involves working with other people. And as you are working with people, you have to be competent at it. A major part of competence is putting similar people and projects together by finding out what people do, what they do best, and what their needs are. And then getting these similar people and projects together which may, or may not, include you. A networker needs to realise that they might not always be a part of the end result or project. However, those connected together by the networker will value, appreciate, and yes, even remember, whoever introduced them and/or suggested that they work together. As you can see, networking is powerful. It is an often invisible, yet tangible resource. You will need to learn and use this resource for continuing collaborations.

Showing competence

> Competence, like truth, beauty, and contact lenses, is in the eye of the beholder. (Laurence J. Peter)

How do you show competence? What actions will make people say of you, 'So and so is very competent'. We think people show competence when they say they will do something, complete it thoroughly and on time, give credit and thanks to all those who helped them, and finally keep everyone involved or interested aware of the progress. Competent people are also willing to change the outcome or work if requested to do so. If you do all of these things then you can be certain that you are showing competence.

So why should we care about competence? If people think that you are competent then they can trust that you do what you say you will, within the given time. They will want to work with you, or hook you up with potential partners because they know that you will hold up your end of the work. Not only will you get the work done that *they* said you would, you then in turn make them look competent, because they recommended you and you were what they said you were – competent. It goes full circle.

It is important to remember, however, that being competent does not mean conforming or giving up your individuality. In fact, if you keep your individuality and show competence, people will appreciate your professionalism and your eccentricities.

> Whoever undertakes to set himself up as a judge of truth and knowledge is shipwrecked by the laughter of the gods. (Albert Einstein)

Openness

> The capacity for fear and for happiness are the same, the unrestricted openness to experience amounting to self-abandonment in which the vanquished rediscovers himself. (Theodor Adorno)

We all have different working styles with often overlapping work ethics and we all excel at different things. When we are open to these differences, great benefits come to us and our organisations. We do not ask you to change your style completely; mostly we are encouraging you to be aware of and accommodating to all the possible different working and communicating styles of your collaborators. Remember, you are trying to get work done together. You are not their boss, and you probably won't write an evaluation of their work. Supposedly, you are helping each other to reach a shared goal. You will have to recognise that because of their differing perspectives, your collaborators will often have very different ways of looking at and approaching problems, and subsequently finding creative solutions. You must be willing to try things you have never tried before – even things that may seem counterintuitive to how you normally work. You will have to trust that your partners are experts in their fields, which often means something very different from being an expert in your own field. So when a partner says, 'this is how it is like for me, or from my perspective,' believe them, and ask how you can help, or barring that, ask for clarification and examples to help gain new perspective.

Being open to new things does not mean that you have to change. However, it might mean that you are more likely to change when a situation demands it.

Technical knowledge

> Every act of conscious learning requires the willingness to suffer an injury to one's self-esteem. That is why young children, before they are aware of their own self-importance, learn so easily; and why older persons, especially if vain or important, cannot learn at all. (Thomas Szasz)

We are in the age where there is a huge need for life-long learning. No one has the luxury of resting on their laurels, especially in the area of technology. No one can afford to stop learning about and how to use new technology skills. Deal with it. Take the course, learn how to use the new software, integrate it into your work. Realise it is a fluid learning process requiring constant refinement and change. Adaptability is the key to success and long-term sustainability. In addition, realise that technology is a tool for getting things done. It is no more and no less than a tool. Treat it as such. You must have the correct tools to get the job done.

Organisational attributes

Some of us have more control or say-so in the organisations for whom we work. However, it makes little difference where we are in the hierarchy, we can still step back and analyse how likely or not collaborations will spring to life where we work. No matter how far down the totem pole we may be, we can manage upward and encourage our supervisors and administrators to change structures and work environments so that we can start collaborating internally and outside of the library walls. Below is a discussion of the various attributes of organisations that contribute to collaborative work.

Supervisory support and freedom

You will need to have, if at all possible, the support from your supervisor before you begin a collaborative project. There are times where this may not be possible, and you will have to do the project on the sly. Should you get positive results, you can then present them to your supervisor and say, 'Look at this collaboration, see the results and see how it builds our relationship with these constituents. In addition, I was able to get all of my other job responsibilities taken care of'. Of course, you will find a much better way to present these ideas to your supervisor that we have stated here!

The best case scenario is to enter into collaborative ventures with the support from your supervisor. This may require a well thought-out and documented plan to get your boss to that point. This can be a major part of the planning process.

It is also advantageous to be given the freedom to collaborate without having to run to your supervisor for the OK on the small details of the project. Time is usually of the essence in collaborative projects, and adding in another level of decision making can bring a collaborative venture to a screeching halt.

> You can't always wait for the guys at the top. Every manager at every level in the organization has an opportunity, big or small, to do something. Every manager's got some sphere of autonomy. Don't pass the buck up the line. (Bob Anderson)

Knowing mutual goals and long-term plans

It can really help collaboration if all parties share their goals in advance of the project, especially when the participants find that there are shared goals. In addition, it is vital to share any thoughts on long-term plans for the outcome of the collaboration. Will you write an article? Together? Will you use the data to compile a dataset to use in long-term strategic planning? Who will be responsible for the deliverables? How will you all define closure? Answering these kinds of questions early in the process, or providing a time to do so at some point in the collaboration can help ensure that there are few, if any, misunderstandings of what, if anything, will happen with the final product of your collaboration.

It also helps for the collaborators to share the long-term goals of their own departments/libraries/institutions as they are relevant to the collaboration. This can often expand the way everyone is thinking about the work they will do together. You can also find out very early if there are conflicting goals that, if not acknowledged early on, could derail the entire collaboration. Remember the more you share at the beginning, the less likely there will be any nasty surprises popping up in the middle of a project.

> Goals provide the energy source that powers our lives. One of the best ways we can get the most from the energy we have is to focus it. That is what goals can do for us; concentrate our energy. (Denis Waitley)

Having the space to do it – physical and virtual

It is very important that each party has the space for working on the collaborative project. On an individual level this could mean a designated paper or electronic folder to store the work of the collaboration, or web space to share documents and information. If there is nowhere for the collaborators to work together or to keep their shared work, this lack of resource will be an obstacle to pursuing the project.

> Form follows function – that has been misunderstood. Form and function should be one, joined in a spiritual union. (Frank Lloyd Wright)

Marketing

People have to know what you do and how you do it before they will want to work with you – word of mouth is the most powerful marketing tool. Be willing to start small and have your collaboration be successful, and it will grow. You have to be willing to talk about your past experiences and then, on your own, come up with new applications of the skills you have learned.

Ideas for marketing:

- give a talk about a project you completed;
- write a paper about it;
- ask the recipients of your last collaborative product for feedback on the work you did with or for them and share that feedback on a web page, or in a newspaper or journal article;
- make posters advertising your classes.

Finally, don't worry if there is not much participation the first time you collaborate. Make sure that the participants felt it was a good experience, and they will want to work with you again, and will tell others how great it was.

The aim of marketing is to know and understand the customer so well the product or service fits him and sells itself. (Peter F. Drucker)

Further reading

While the majority of these readings focus on marketing, you will find a few on networking, social skills at work, professionalism, and other attributes of good collaborators.

Adams, K. E. and Cassner M. E. (2001) 'Marketing library resources and services to distance faculty at the University of Nebraska-Lincoln'. *Journal of Library Administration* 31(3/4): 5–22.

Anonymous. (2005) 'Five common networking mistakes to avoid'. *Design Firm Management & Administration Report* 05(8): 2–3.

Anonymous. (2005) 'The art of getting connected'. *Strategic Direction* 21(8): 9.

Archer, S. B. (2001) '"Be all that you can be": developing and marketing professionalism in academic reference librarianship'. *The Reference Librarian* 73: 351–60.

Ashcroft, L. (2002) 'Issues in developing, managing and marketing electronic journals collections'. *Collection Building* 21(4): 147–54.

Bainbridge, J. (1998) 'Social skills add to job chances'. *Marketing*: 51.

Block, J. and Edzan N. N. (2002) 'Information marketing in Sri Lankan academic libraries'. *Malaysian Journal of Library & Information Science* 7(2): 87–100.

Brong, J. (2005) 'Take center stage'. *Quality Progress* 38(7): 75.

Crocker, J. L. (1994) 'Marketing, public relations and the academic library'. *New Jersey Libraries* 27: 6.

Cruickshank, J. L. and Nowak D. G. (2001) 'Marketing reference resources and services through a university outreach program at Mississippi State University'. *The Reference Librarian* 73: 265–80.

D'Andraia, F. (1994) 'The business of libraries is staying in business: academic libraries must develop marketing plans to reach customers'. *Journal of Library Administration* 20(2): 81–91.

Delima, F. (2005) 'Want a strong career? Start nurturing those weak ties'. *Computing Canada* 31(3): 31.

Demers, J. (2002) 'Networking to advance your career'. *CMA Management* 76(1): 11.

Dodsworth, E. M. (1998) 'Marketing academic libraries: a necessary plan'. *The Journal of Academic Librarianship* 24(4): 320–2.

Dugdale, D. and Dugdale, C. (2000) 'Growing an electronic library: resources, utility, marketing and politics. ResIDe electronic library at the University of the West of England'. *Journal of Documentation* 56(6): 644–59.

Ekpenyong, G. D. (2003) 'Marketing and promotion of information services in the University of Ibadan Library'. *Information Development* 19(3): 197–202.

Furlong, K. and Crawford, A. B. (1999) 'Marketing your services through your students at the University of Maine at Farmington'. *Computers in Libraries* 19(8): 22–4.

Gaspar, S. (2001) 'Management strategies: Successful schmoozing'. *Network World* 18(44): 53.

Giesecke, J., Egbers, G. and Logan-Peters K. (1990) 'Marketing without a plan: seizing outreach opportunities as they appear'. *Nebraska Library Association Quarterly* 21: 5–10.

Gupta-Sunderji, M. (2004) 'Power networking'. *CGA Magazine* 38(3): 36.

Hart, J. L., Coleman, V. and Yu, H. (1999) 'Marketing electronic resources and services: surveying faculty use as a first step at Texas A&M University'. *The Reference Librarian* 67/68: 41–55.

Houston, J. R. (1993) 'Marketing your library: an outreach plan for Ohio Wesleyan University's depository library collection'. *Library Mosaics* 4: 15.

Jackson, M. (2001) 'Marketing the HyLiFe project in UK academic libraries'. *Library Management* 22(1/2): 43–9.

LaGuardia, C. M. and Martorana, J. (1993) 'Marketing the library: the library media fair. University of California, Santa Barbara'. *College & Research Libraries News* 9: 502.

Landrum, M. C. (1987) 'Marketing library services to faculty'. *Colorado Libraries* 13: 15–16.

Lawson, M. D. (1999) 'Reaching the masses: marketing a library instruction course to incoming freshmen. at Central Missouri State University'. *Research Strategies* 17(1): 45–9.

LeBeau, C. (1999) 'Marketing basics in a changing information age: interview with professor of marketing John Workman'. *Nebraska Library Association Quarterly* 30(4): 3–11.

Martey, A. K. (2000) 'Marketing products and services of academic libraries in Ghana'. *Libri* 50(4): 261–8.

McDonald, Robert H., Sears, J. and Mitchell, C. (2000) 'Footballs and URLs: marketing your library and its online presence. Library promotion at home football games at Auburn University'. *Computers in Libraries* 20(8): 44–8.

Nims, J. K. (1999) 'Marketing library instruction services: changes and trends'. *Reference Services Review* 27(3): 249–53.

Ramsey, R. D. (2004) 'What's new in networking'. *SuperVision* 65(4): 6–8.

Rozum, B. and Brewer, K. (1997) 'Identifying, developing, and marketing library services to cooperative extension personnel at Utah State University'. *Reference & User Services Quarterly* 37(2): 161–9.

Ryan, L. (2004) 'Nine tips for networking into your next job'. *The Canadian Manager* 29(4): 11–12.

Sparrow, S. (2005) 'Work your way up the career ladder'. *Personnel Today*: 21.

Spiegel, S. and Kinikin J. (2004) 'Promoting geographic information system usage across campus'. *Computers in Libraries* 24(5): 10–16.

Swaine, C. W. (2001) 'Developing, marketing, and evaluating Web-based library and information skills tutorials at Old Dominion University'. *Virginia Libraries* 47(3): 5–8.

Teuton, L. B. (1990) 'Marketing the college library'. *College & Research Libraries News* 11: 1073–4.

Thesing, J. I. (1985) 'Marketing academic library bibliographic instruction programs: case and commentary'. *Research Strategies* 3: 29–36.

Trojahn, L. (1999) 'University libraries are prime for cause-related marketing: partnerships with for-profit organizations at the University of New Mexico'. *Mississippi Libraries* 63(2): 31–5.

Ward, P. L. (2003) 'Continuing professional development and workplace learning 4: Conferences, wonderful conferences'. *Library Management* 24(6/7): 367.

Wolpert, A. J. (1998) 'Services to remote users: marketing the library's role'. *Library Trends* 47(1): 21–41.

Woolley, S. (2001) 'Get connected'. *Money*: 74–82.

3

Technology tools for collaborations

What is a 'technology tool'?

> Technology is so much fun but we can drown in our technology. The fog of information can drive out knowledge. (Daniel J. Boorstin)

In part, current ideas about what constitutes 'technology' depend on what is new and exciting. Many historians of science will argue that the printing press – à la Gutenberg – is a technology that continues to influence the world, yet few 'regular' people would list books among the top technology products in their lives. This chapter examines a number of technologies – defined as computer-based or computer-enabled hardware and software – that assist researchers and educators in their collaborative communication endeavours. The chapter proceeds from e-mail (itself, like the book, rapidly decreasing in 'technology' status) through such hot topics as wikis, blogs, smartboards, videoconferencing, and extremely high-tech visualisation walls.

Before taking a tour through our favourite collaborative tools, however, it would be helpful to take a moment to talk about the fractured landscape that we face. The only thing linking all of these technologies together is their end purpose – facilitating collaboration and communication. Otherwise, there is no unifying principle. Instead, there are a number of dichotomous axes on which we can map the tools. These involve *when* people communicate, *how* people receive information, and *where* the tool is located. Of course, a final axis – *how much* the technology costs to implement and/or use – is a bit trickier to arrange in a pure dichotomy.

It is hard to check five e-mail inboxes, three voice mail systems, or five blogs that you are tracking. (David Rose)

Dichotomy 1: synchronous vs. asynchronous communication (when)

At this point in time many people are familiar with the concept of synchronicity in communication. This gets to whether people are talking to each other at (roughly) the same time, or whether they are going back and forth over a broad period. Historically, this is the difference between talking to your mother and corresponding with her via the postal service. Most collaborators now use some mixture of 'real-time' and delayed communication tools, including meetings, e-mail, and websites (Table 3.1).

Table 3.1 Synchronous vs. asynchronous communication

Synchronous	Asynchronous
Face-to-face meeting	Letters
Telephone	E-mail
Chat	Websites
Wikis (sometimes)	Course management systems
	Blogs
Videoconference	Wikis (sometimes)

| Table 3.2 | Push technologies *vs.* pull technologies |

Push technologies	Pull technologies
E-mail	Websites
Chat	Course management systems
Videoconference	Blogs
	Wikis

Dichotomy 2: push vs. pull (how)

We are fairly used to the idea of e-mail as a 'push' technology, while websites are a 'pull' technology. But what does this mean? The difference is in how people get information, particularly in what they have to do to get it. Push technologies deliver content *to* the (usually) reader whether they want it or not; pull technologies provide content *for* the reader to access on their own (Table 3.2). With a push technology, one can be fairly sure that the other person at least had an opportunity to see your information (although they may not have read their e-mail); with a pull technology one knows that the reader probably wanted to get to you in the first place. Push technologies tend to be very quick while pull technologies tend to be very durable.

Dichotomy 3: software vs. hardware (where)

The next dichotomy is between where the technology 'lives' – whether as a physical object that has to be housed somewhere, or as a virtual piece of software that can be accessed from any location (Table 3.3). Again, this division makes sense to many people.

Table 3.3 Software *vs.* hardware

Software tools	Hardware tools
E-mail	Smartboards
Chat	Videoconferencing (sometimes)
Websites	Visualisation systems
Blogs	
Wikis	
Course management programmes	
Videoconferencing (sometimes)	

Dichotomy 4: cheap *vs.* expensive (how much?)

Finally, the cost to implement each of these technologies has to be taken into account for any academic unit – library or not – considering building collaborative relationships. Note that e-mail and websites are included in the 'cheap' side – this is because the infrastructure for these programmes generally already exists in most universities. Thus, the only real cost to collaborators or facilitators is the cost of learning the software and sending the messages. As mentioned above, it would be more appropriate to list these tools along a continuum from cheap to expensive or easy to hard. They are so arranged in Table 3.4.

Table 3.4 Cheap *vs.* expensive

Cheap	Expensive
E-mail	Course management systems
Chat	Smartboards
Websites	Videoconferencing
Blogs	Visualisation systems
Wikis	

The top tools for collaboration

> The tools I need for my work are paper, tobacco, food, and a little whiskey. (William Faulkner)

E-mail

Most professionals have now had access to e-mail in some form or another for at least ten years; many of us have had access for much longer. At this point e-mail is the type of ubiquitous technology that it may seem surprising to see it listed as a 'collaborative technology'. E-mail has its strengths and weaknesses, most of which have been hashed over many times in the literature, in magazines, and on the news. Despite the problems that we see with e-mail, it is a technology that is here to stay.

Why? Because it is quick, cheap, easily shared with multiple people, and time- and space-independent. This makes it an ideal way for collaborators in different locations and on different schedules to share information without direct contact. E-mail is excellent for basic tasks, such as scheduling and for file transfer, ideation, and some limited discussion of issues. However, some newer technologies have emerged that should supplement e-mail as a communication and collaboration tool.

> I only got one e-mail from a prisoner, which kind of surprised me that they have computers in prison. (Cindy Margolis)

Chat

One of the long running complaints with e-mail – in addition to one of its strengths – is that the writer of an e-mail has to wait for the recipient to log into their e-mail, read the message, and write a reply. A conversation over e-mail both takes a long time and clutters up the inbox with short messages. Even something as simple as choosing a location for a meeting can take several hours of messages flying back and forth. Many people eventually resort to the telephone to accomplish short conversations. However, even that technology only works if both people are at known phone numbers and have the time to talk. What about the person telecommuting from home, or working on several tasks at once?

Enter chat. Known to our younger patrons by various brand names – AIM, ICQ, and Netscape Messenger – these simple software programs allow a user to register (usually for free) and log into the shared chat space. If you are on the same system as the person with whom you wish to chat and know their chat name (these can be pretty creative), you can open up a shared window with them. In libraries we are also familiar with chat software that allows cobrowsing of websites and archiving of transcripts, such as the products from LSSI and Docutek. However, many libraries are abandoning those expensive products in favour of setting up an AIM account for 'libraryrefdesk'.

Chat has, of course, been around as a supporting tool for online classes, 'virtual reference', and Internet gaming for a long time. Its strength as an independent collaboration tool lies in its utility for quick online meetings, including preliminary data sharing and progress checks. However, chat will likely persist in the scholarly arena in its supporting role to other types of shared meeting space, including videoconferencing (discussed later in this chapter).

> Most people are awaiting Virtual Reality; I'm awaiting virtuous reality. (Eli Khamarov)

Websites

In the autumn of 2005 one of the older web browsers, Opera, celebrated its tenth anniversary. Like e-mail, most professionals have enough familiarity with the Internet and with using websites that they hardly consider 'The Web' to be a technology any more. While designers have become very good at presenting graphics, text, and even streaming video and audio over web browsers, these sites are essentially limited in the kind of collaboration that they allow. As the epitome of an online pull technology, websites have functioned very well for presenting relatively static information. Collaborators typically set up a website with contact and biographical information for the participants, meeting schedules, and links to descriptions of research, published papers, and presentations. However, as creating a typical website requires at least some knowledge of HTML as well as access to a server, these sites are usually controlled by one or two members of the team (or their staff) who have the time, skills, and permissions to update content. These weaknesses are beginning to be addressed in two emerging technologies, blogs and wikis.

> So many celebrity websites you go to are so sterile that you know they just pay somebody to do it and there's not even an ounce of them in it. (Cindy Margolis)

Blogs

The use of the Internet for maintaining a journal or diary of one's activities – known as 'web logs' or simply 'blogs' - has been common practice among the Millennial generation for years. Only recently, however, have researchers started using these systems for scholarly work. At their core, blogs enable one or several people to put up short notes on the Internet quickly and easily, and in some instances allow other people to comment on those notes. No knowledge of HTML is necessary for posting to the blog, which makes participation in it even less of a burden to the non-technologically inclined.

Blogs are taking the place of e-mail communication for notices that need to be communicated to a large group of people quickly – but that also have persistent relevance. Because these messages are posted to a common site, rather than pushed to individual e-mail accounts, they can be easily archived and searched in the future. In essence, the blog is a melding of the posting, archiving, and searching functions available in websites with the ease of creation of e-mail. From the creator's perspective, this is an ideal technology when the need arises to communicate something that is either too short or too time-sensitive to warrant a full website.

On the other hand, blogs are a pull technology, meaning that readers have to have chosen to navigate to the blog to read the information. Push technologies, like e-mail and paper mail, are sent out to the reader – but of course, the recipient can always choose to ignore the message that is sent. In other words, blogs present a slight barrier to information on the reader's side, as the reader must first know about the blog and navigate to it in order to get the content.

Examples of appropriate uses of blogs for scholarly work:

- shared laboratory (or other group) notebook;
- logging completion of steps in a task with sharing of affiliated information;
- communication between collaborators;

- tips, notes, and events;

- departmental, group, or individual news.

Compared with either websites or e-mails, one major difference of the scholarly blog is the option to open it up to comments from either the general public or a restricted group of users. An example would be a main posting that discusses a new protocol for a biomedical procedure, which can then be discussed by laboratory or clinical group members via the blog's commenting function. E-mail newsgroups sometimes accomplish this function – though rarely well – via replies to previous e-mail postings. The blog, however, has the advantage of keeping all of the comments in one location, and in order of time of posting. They are generally easier to read than the typical online discussion group, as well, and allow for hyperlinking to other websites and blogs, or to other content.

> First, I'd become an avid reader of blogs, especially music blogs, and they seemed to be where the critical-thinking action was at, to have the kind of energy that I associate with rock writing of the 1970s or Internet e-mail discussion lists a decade ago. (Carl Wilson)

Wikis

Another take on enhancing the static, one-creator-at-a-time website is the development of the wiki. From the Hawaiian word for fast, *wiki wiki,* the wiki was first created by as a tool for multi-authorship of online content. The most commonly known example is the Wikipedia (*http://www. wikipedia.com*), an online encyclopaedia that has literally hundreds of authors all writing about what they know (or think they know) best.

Wikis work by allowing write-access to either the general public or to a select set of users by password. Every writer with the appropriate permissions can log into the wiki at any time and change content – by reformatting, adding or deleting text, or even adding/deleting whole pages of content. Previous versions are usually archived along with notes about the changes made, just in case a reversion is desired. This is an exciting new technology with many applications in scholarly work, including:

- shared authoring/editing of manuscripts, including articles, grants, working papers, etc.;
- shared authoring/editing of scholarly websites;
- shared knowledge bases, including thesauri, glossaries, and encyclopaedias.

The great power of the wiki is that it eliminates the need to send working files to colleagues, wait for revisions, collate revisions into one document, send out the revised document, get new revisions, collate the new revisions, and so on. With the wiki, group members simply log in to see the most recently revised document/website/etc., and amend content as they see fit. As successive versions are archived, the current editor can look up what was most recently changed. There is no longer a problem with version control or lost edits.

There are, of course, problems with allowing anyone to edit a document. All parties may not agree with changes made – leading to a battle over who edits the paper last. In addition, opening up your wiki to the general public can lead to spam and other inappropriate content being posted. However, the example of the Wikipedia shows that, in general, moderation wins in this kind of shared creative space.

We talked about the Internet and Wikipedia and how facts and history are being collectively created online. (Joichi Ito)

Course management systems

The various course management systems (including Blackboard and WebCT), allow instructors to create an online space for their classes within a templatised shell. As with wikis and blogs, this limits the amount of coding necessary for providing professional-level content while also enabling faculty to update and modify content as needed. In addition, courses can be held completely online using these systems. Either the course may be run asynchronously – through the use of narrated presentations and readings with electronic drop boxes for assignments – or faculty may choose to use the chat and 'office hours' options available. A major advantage of these systems is that they allow faculty to manage a piece of a course independently from the rest of the course, while maintaining a consistent look and feel. This can be very helpful for courses that are team-taught or rely heavily on guest lecturers, including librarians. Indeed, many students now expect – and prefer – electronic 'handouts' via their course page rather than in print format.

> Education is not a problem. Education is an opportunity. (Lyndon B. Johnson)

Smartboards

One of the long-time tools for collaboration has been a system for writing on a vertical surface using different colours. At first this would have been a chalkboard, followed, over time, by the flip chart and whiteboard. An inherent weakness of each of these tools is the inability to easily capture what was written, share it with participants, and archive it for later reference. New technologies using electronic pens and tracking systems are making it possible to save and print copies of notes written on either existing whiteboards or on specially-designed 'smartboards'.

In the simplest version, special cameras are attached to the corners of an existing whiteboard, and special pens are substituted for the standard dry-wipe marker pens.

A special overlay is also available for plasma screens. In this case, a special screen is added onto the front of the plasma television, and the system is connected to the computer using the plasma screen as a monitor. When notes are made on the screen, they are electronically transmitted via the overlay system to the computer which 'draws' them on the desktop. No actual ink is in the pens.

The third version of a smartboard technology is the true SmartBoard. This system uses ink pens that also have an RF connection to a computer. The board can function like a normal whiteboard, but it can also connect with your computer in order to save the image on the board, connect with a projector system to make notes on a website, document, etc., and/or archive the notes as an image file.

> But it is strange how many rational beings believe the ultimate truths of the universe to be reducible to patterns on a blackboard. (Frederick Pollock)

Videoconferencing

It may have once been the case that collaborators on a project were geographically close enough to meet face to face – or they may have accepted that travel was a necessary part of collaboration with colleagues at differing institutions. In-person meetings are rapidly becoming less important to successful collaborative ventures as audio- and videoconferencing technologies have improved.

In the simplest scenario, a number of collaborators may call into a shared telephone line. This standard teleconference technology works just fine if you only need to discuss something but don't need to work in real time on a project, share data, or see the other person or people. It is, of course, possible to dial into a teleconference while at the same time work in real time on the project wiki, but this starts getting a bit complicated.

The standard protocol for Internet-based videoconferencing, using a web-camera and (in the best case) T1 line, is the NISO H.323. This standard allows for video and audio to be transmitted across the Internet to multiple locations. Various software programs control the audio and visual streams. Some software also enables real-time file-sharing.

Another option for videoconferencing in a fixed location is participation in the AccessGrid (AG). This system uses dedicated cameras and computing on proprietary software to share audio, video, and data. The AG is very popular in academic and US government institutions as well as major research institutions around the world. Unlike H.323 videoconferencing, AG systems can only talk with other AG systems, which can limit their utility for small collaborations.

> A conference is a gathering of people who singly can do nothing, but together can decide that nothing can be done. (Fred A. Allen)

Visualisation technologies

Most researchers are probably only ever exposed to visualisation as a possibility on their laptop monitors – which may be one of the driving forces behind the push to higher and higher resolution flat screen systems. There are, however, a number of extremely high-end systems that allow scientists, in particular, to display visual information in a collaboration-enabled way.

One such system is a VisWall as produced by Visbox, Inc. In its current installation, a VisWall is an eight by ten foot, sixteen screen, rear-projected visual display system. The major feature of such display 'walls' is that they are able to increase the pixels per inch to a resolution far superior to any current monitor and almost all conventional projections systems. Another major feature is that, as the images are projected from behind the screen, collaborators can stand in front of the image being discussed without casting a shadow on the wall. The combination of these three features produces a technology that enables the sharing and discussion of high-density visual data, such as annotated genetic sequences, molecular models, PET scans, topological data, and so on.

There are relatively few visual display systems in use in the USA at this time – and only a handful that are associated with university libraries. The display wall in the University of North Carolina-Chapel Hill Health Sciences Library's Collaboration Center is a joint project of the Health Sciences Library and the Renaissance Computing Institute (RENCI), which is itself a joint venture of three academic institutions in North Carolina. This partnership arose largely as a matter of economics. The wall itself is very expensive, particularly for a library, and requires demand from a very broad user population to justify the cost. RENCI was in possession of key elements of the hardware and expertise, but had no appropriate location in which to install the wall. The Library provides both an excellent central location and a strong desire to be a partner in such collaborative enterprises as the wall facilitates; RENCI provides the hardware and at least initial support for the software used on the wall.

> Visualize, 'prayerize', 'actionize', and your wishes will come true. (Charles L. Allen)

The library's role

Each of these technologies offers a different perspective on collaboration in scholarly research and education. Several are currently in use in the average library and university, while others are only popular among the extremely savvy or very well financially endowed. Libraries, as both a neutral space (physical, virtual, and emotional) and a centre for information science expertise, can and should provide the leadership on campus that is necessary for incorporating these technologies into academic life.

Provide space: physical and virtual

There is currently a building boom among US academic libraries, both to create new facilities and to renovate existing ones. Many of these libraries are working to re-evaluate their position and purpose in the academic sphere. Increasingly, libraries are creating collaborative study, research, and teaching spaces to attract interest from their constituencies. These physical spaces may be as simple as a room with a table and a whiteboard, or as complex as a full collaboration centre with a visualisation wall, smartboard, access grid node, and computer workstations. Virtual space is also important. The library may provide servers to support blogs and wikis, or simply links on the homepage to videoconferencing resources and calendars.

Provide expertise

Library and information professionals are uniquely skilled to identify, implement, and promote novel collaborative technologies for the general academic community. Between reference staff, who can investigate the applicability of tools to each situation and systems staff, who may be asked to implement and/or consult on projects involving software and hardware installations, the library can and should be a partner with the university community by supplying the information needed to use the tools most effectively.

Provide leadership

Above all else, the libraries have an opportunity – and the responsibility – to take a leadership role in the university setting. Research and teaching departments may be too involved in their individual programmes to consider novel communication and collaboration tools, much less to evaluate and implement them in a test setting.

> Big companies have entire departments that manage these kinds of solutions ... this is a new high-water mark for small businesses that want to improve collaboration thanks to the tight integration of Exchange 2003, SharePoint and Outlook. (Robert Hamilton)

Further reading

Much research being done on the role of technology in the collaborative process, as well as how tools like wikis and blogs are used for scholarly communication. Whole conferences exist to show off the latest 'collaboration technology'.

Chang, M. (2004) 'I've gathered a basket of communication and collaboration tools'. *Computers in Libraries* 24(8): 6–8, 61–2.

Clyde, L. A. (2004) *Weblogs and Libraries.* Oxford: Chandos Publishing.

Daw, M. (2005) 'Advanced collaboration with the access grid'. *Ariadne*: 42.

Fichter, D. (2005). 'The many forms of e-collaboration: Blogs, wikis, portals, groupware, discussion boards, and instant messaging'. *Online* 29(4): 48–50.

Frumkin, J. (2005) 'The wiki and the digital library'. *OCLC Systems & Services* 21(1): 18–22.

Heath, C., Hindmarsh, J., Kuzuoka, H., Luff, P., Oyama, S. and Yamazaki, K. (2003) 'Fractured ecologies: Creating environments for collaboration'. *Human–Computer Interaction* 18(1–2): 51–84.

Lueg, C. and Fisher, D. (eds) (2003) *From Usenet to CoWebs: Interacting with Social Information Spaces.* London: Springer-Verlag,

Mays, A. (2003) 'Biz of Acq – using technology to increase collaboration between the library, teaching faculty, and the campus at large'. *Against the Grain* 15(5): 74–78.

Sochrin, S. (2004) 'Learning to teach in a new medium: Adapting library instruction to a videoconferencing environment'. *Journal of Library Administration* 41: 429–442.

4

Getting started

Introduction

> Being busy does not always mean real work. The object
> of all work is production or accomplishment and to
> either of these ends there must be forethought, system,
> planning, intelligence, and honest purpose, as well as
> perspiration. Seeming to do is not doing. (Thomas Alva
> Edison)

If our work responsibilities were strictly confined to what
was listed on our job descriptions, many of us would feel
bored and unchallenged at work. We would probably soon
be unable to do our jobs very well, or perhaps not be able to
do them at all. Our users and their needs are constantly
changing, so if we don't change along with them we will not
have the skills necessary to cope in the new work
environment that this change brings. Fortunately, working
on collaborative projects can offer us new challenges beyond
those of our routine workday. It allows us to solve problems
that go beyond the scope of a single individual's job
responsibilities by working with others. Further, it also
allows us to solve common problems or issues that are often
not confined solely to our individual departments, libraries,
or institutions. Hopefully, you have already been sold on the
benefits of working collaboratively if you have read the

earlier chapters. But the nagging questions remains: How do you start working on a collaboration? What are the steps in the process that will keep the project on track and moving forward? This chapter looks at assembling the framework for collaboration – agreeing on the project, gathering participants, running meetings, marshalling tools and skills, and getting support.

> Individual commitment to a group effort – that is what makes a team work, a company work, a society work, a civilization work. (Vince Lombardi)

Agreeing on the project

Many collaborative projects evolve out of an identified need to solve recurring problems we are experiencing at work. For example, you might get students from an undergraduate history class coming into your library every term right before final papers are due. They need your help because they must have primary sources in their bibliographies, but they are unsure of what a primary source is and how to go about finding them in the library. Or, from talking to faculty in your subject area, you might find that their students don't know how to acknowledge the work of other writers in their papers. They complain that plagiarism is rampant: students borrow the ideas and writings of others without citing them. Both examples highlight issues that could be addressed through collaborative projects. In the first example, how to get history students to distinguish between primary and secondary sources of literature and how do you teach them to find primary sources in the library? In the second example, how do you teach students to acknowledge the ideas of others in the text and references of their papers?

Agreeing to work on a collaborative project with the faculty or with other librarians, can be the answer to these recurring problems. But before you can begin, you must find your collaborators, define your audience, and determine your end product.

Having clearly identified a shared problem is a good first step towards a successful collaboration. First and foremost, it helps you to identify possible collaborators. In the case of the history students, an obvious partner could be the teacher of the class. The two of you will probably agree that there is a significant need to teach the students how to identify and find primary sources, and that doing this during class time and making it part of their course requirements will get the students to take the library instruction seriously. If there is no collaboration between you and the teacher, you will get stuck showing each student individually and the teacher won't have access to your subject and searching expertise in showing the students what to do. Collaboration will save not only your time and the teacher's time, but also it will save the students' time. In the second example, there is clear need to teach students how to acknowledge the work of others in the papers so they don't plagiarise. Possible collaborators could be faculty members who had problems with plagiarism in the past or other librarians who have helped students with their citations. If you know your problem, it will help you know your fellow collaborators.

With your problem clearly identified, you can also start to determine your intended audience or audiences. Knowing and then describing your audience before you begin may seem obvious as an early activity, but unfortunately many collaborations are begun too quickly and, therefore, are designed without much consideration of what the audience is like, and what the best ways to communicate with them may be. For example, imagine trying to create an online tutorial on how to find and use psychology resources in the library. The original idea is that the online tutorial will appeal to undergraduates, graduate students, and faculty. An analysis of the audience, however, will show that it is not possible for this tutorial to be all things to all people.

If you create an in-depth list and discussion of psychology resources, this tutorial will be useful for faculty and graduate students but will be overkill, and ignored by, most undergraduates. However, if you use your tutorial to describe the differences between primary and secondary sources in psychology, it will be helpful to undergraduates, but will be insulting to more advanced researchers like graduate students and faculty. As this example illustrates, the danger in trying to make your project reach a varied audience, is that you wind up with a result that pleases no one. It is important to have a targeted audience and impress that one focused group. This way you make at least one audience happy and the possibility exists that you might impress other audiences also.

Now that you have figured out your audience, you can determine what form the end product of your collaboration should take. When doing this you will want to make sure that your final results will match the skills, expectations, and learning styles of that audience. A tutorial mounted on the Web, designed to interact with the end user might be perfectly appropriate for tech savvy undergraduates. The same tutorial might cause confusion and never get used at all if it were intended for octogenarians. On the other hand, if these same senior citizens have taken computer classes, then the tutorial might be a good fit with their skills and needs.

> I dream of a collaboration that would finally be total, in which the librettist would often think as a composer and the composer as a librettist. (Jacques Ibert)

Soliciting participants

> It is probably not love that makes the world go around, but rather those mutually supportive alliances through which partners recognize their dependence on each other for the achievement of shared and private goals. (Fred Allen)

So you've come up with a great idea for a project that you know will be well received by your target audience. You've identified possible collaborators who can help you make your project a reality. Now you have to turn these 'possible' collaborators into partners. With work demands being what they are, this is often easier said than done. Soliciting participants for your project is when you really need to sell the benefits of working on a collaboration.

These benefits can vary depending on who your fellow collaborators are and what the project will involve. Collaborating with colleagues from your library can have obvious work-related perks. Joining up with colleagues can greatly improve and increase your day-to-day contacts. You will find out what is going on in other departments and consequently you will gain a better understanding of the work environments throughout the organisation. Making these sorts of partnerships often pays huge dividends for you and your collaborators long after the project is complete.

Collaborating with staff from other libraries has its perks. The most important of these is networking opportunities, which is handy if, say, you decide to re-enter the job market after having been away for any number of reasons. Working with staff from other libraries also allows you to see how others respond to problems that are shared by all libraries. For example, you can find out how other libraries are handling the high cost of their journal subscriptions, or how they are managing their growing digital assets. This sharing of knowledge might not be germane to your project at the time, but it will give you and your collaborators a better understanding of how librarianship is practised at different institutions.

Collaborating with faculty is a desirable partnership as faculty are an important part of your user or customer base. Along with working together on the project, you will have the opportunity to assess the library needs of the faculty you are collaborating with. This can give you an idea of how well your library's services and collections are meeting faculty expectations and needs. Partnering with faculty also gives you entrée for future outreach opportunities, such as providing library instruction in the classroom. These collaborations can benefit your library as well, because faculty are powerful allies in the world of the university.

When soliciting participants for your project, you should be honest with them about time commitments up front. Although a particular collaboration might be wonderful and truly needed, participants in it will quickly lose enthusiasm if takes up half of their working week and they weren't expecting that kind of time commitment. If a project is expected to take up plenty of time and effort, it can be helpful for participants to get permission from their supervisors before they join the collaboration.

Meetings

Meetings are a great trap. Soon you find yourself trying to get agreement and then the people who disagree come to think they have a right to be persuaded. However, they are indispensable when you don't want to do anything. (John Kenneth Galbraith)

Thanks to technology, a lot of collaborative work that used to be done face-to-face can now be done remotely. With tools such as e-mail and wikis, it is not necessary for these physical meetings to take place. Many collaborations flourish and succeed without the participants ever having a face-to-face encounter. Work can be posted, reviewed, and edited without project participants having to leave their offices. This does not, however, completely eliminate the need for meetings. They're needed for brainstorming ideas when it's important to have a critical mass of thinking. Meetings are also useful for keeping track of the project and making sure all the participants are up-to-date. Meetings are vital if the number of collaborators is greater than three or four. Finally, a meeting is nice when you and you collaborators have finished the project and it's time to celebrate. You could drink champagne alone in your office but it's more fun to do it together with your partners.

Planning meetings does require a little bit of logistical legwork. Generally, you will have to reserve a room in your library or department (unless you are fortunate enough to have a really large office). If you are working on an online or digital project, you will have to reserve a computer lab or be able to access a laptop and projector. If you are partnering with colleagues from other libraries and they are driving over to your school, it is extremely helpful if you can find them parking spaces. Collaborations lose their appeal if your collaborators get parking tickets. If you don't know how to obtain a room, computing equipment, or parking spaces, now is good time to go talk the administrative assistant in your library or library system. They know about these activities, as well as lots of other useful information. Being kind to administrative assistants is critical if you want to succeed as a collaborator, as well if you want to succeed as a librarian!

Make a habit of rotating who is responsible for planning and arranging the meetings. If one participant is always stuck organising the meetings, they will probably tire of it very quickly. Being responsible for taking and sending out the minutes of the meetings can also quickly grow old, so plan on rotating those duties also. Make sure everyone has their turn with this task.

Setting ground rules

> Rules are for the obedience of fools and the guidance of wise men. (Douglas Bader)

Collaborations have the best chance for success when all participants agree to a series of ground rules at the start of the project. The following rules can help you get started in coming up with your own:

- *Attend all meetings*: if you can't make it to a meeting, find out if there is something else you can do to contribute to the project; don't let your absence excuse you or keep others from making progress on the project.

- *Come prepared*: if you are unprepared, you are wasting the time of your collaborators. Go over the agenda prior to attending the meeting; make sure you have read and reviewed all pertinent documents so you can contribute at the meeting.

- *Agree on communication formats and guidelines on acceptable use*: decide the best way for project participants to communicate with one another. For most groups, e-mail works well for keeping track of the project and for posting work; make sure all communication is shared with everyone in the group; if all the members are up to date with correspondence, this saves time by not having to bring individuals up to speed.

- *Listen respectfully*: if you want your ideas to be considered seriously by the group, you should do the same for others – don't interrupt group members; wait until they have finished speaking their point.

- *Be willing to compromise*: compromising is essential to working collaboratively. If you aren't willing to compromise, you should probably work on your project alone.

Creating the timeline

A schedule defends from chaos and whim. It is a net for catching days. It is a scaffolding on which a worker can stand and labor with both hands at sections of time. (Annie Dillard)

At the beginning of a collaboration it can be difficult to estimate how long your project will take to complete. If you allot yourself too little time at the outset of a project, you and your fellow collaborators will be constantly battling deadlines and won't have time to respond to any changes that inevitably pop up during any project. On the other hand, if you allot yourselves too much time to complete the work, many of you may lose track of the project and end up procrastinating away all the extra time. Coming up with a balanced schedule that allows for unplanned contingencies, yet keeps everyone moving towards the goal is key for creating a successful project timeline.

When creating a timeline, divide your project into separate tasks. For example, if you are creating an online guide designed to show library users the difference between primary and secondary resources, you might break up your project into the following steps:

- analysing other online guides;
- writing up content for the guide;
- editing the content;
- designing the website and posting the content to it;
- testing the website;
- advertising website.

By breaking the project into separate tasks, you can assign deadlines for each task instead of just having one deadline for the whole project. Having separate deadlines for individual tasks will help keep you all on track and provide opportunities for checks and balances as the project proceeds. Meeting these smaller deadlines can also provide a sense of accomplishment throughout the project.

Instead of setting firm dates for your deadlines, give yourselves a range of time to complete the separate tasks. For example, you could predict that a particular task will take three to five weeks to complete instead of having a firm four-week deadline. This flexible time range gives everyone the opportunity to deal with surprises, which, as we all know, will more than likely occur during your collaboration.

Tools for the project

> Man is a tool-using animal. Nowhere do you find him without tools; without tools he is nothing, with tools he is all. (Thomas Carlyle)

You can't paint a picture without a brush; likewise, it is also hard to collaborate on a project without the proper tools. It is important to have technological support both to facilitate the project and to create the end product of the collaboration. Below is a brief discussion of the technology available to use for collaboration – see Chapter 3 for an in-depth discussion of technology tools for communication and work sharing.

When working on the project, technology can be employed by group members to communicate. Much of this communication can and probably will take the form of e-mail, which is accessible to almost all who work in academic libraries. Wikis make it possible for collaborators to easily post work and have it reviewed and edited by other group members via the Web. Blogs allow group members to communicate and post their work. Instant messaging offers real-time communication for remote group members. Project management software can be used to facilitate and manage the entire collaborative process.

Technology needs can vary widely in collaborations when it comes to presenting or posting the end product of the group. If the end product is an online guide, it is necessary for at least one member of the collaboration to have web-authoring tools available for their use as well being able to access server space to mount the website. If the end product is a library instruction session, chances are you will need access to a computer lab. It is important to determine what technology your group will need for the final product early in the planning stages of your collaboration.

People for the project

> Problems can become opportunities when the right people come together. (Robert South)

Matching the skills of the people involved with the tasks they are able to do, or can learn how to do, is probably even more critical to your collaboration than the technology. You will have to think about the steps involved in the project and consider who is best suited to complete each task. As a project can involve multiple tasks (e.g. research, content writing, editing, implementing technology, usability testing), collaborating is an opportunity to bring together people who may have a wide array of skills. You will probably have to look beyond your normal colleagues to assemble the group. However, the nature of the project will ultimately dictate who you recruit. You must be willing to look far and wide for appropriate collaborators. For example, if you are a subject librarian, don't automatically recruit other subject librarians. Consider the skills that can be brought to your project by other groups, such as instructional librarians, IT specialists, cataloguers, paraprofessionals, faculty, or students. In addition, you will want to consider recruiting staff from other institutions. This works best if your project can satisfy a shared need.

Collaboration offers you and your partners the opportunity to try out skills that you might not have or that you don't get to use in your day-to-day work. For example, an IT specialist might want to write content for a tutorial or a subject librarian might want to perform usability testing on a website. Be flexible in allowing group members to try out new roles and skills.

The final result

Work joyfully and peacefully, knowing that right thoughts and right efforts inevitably bring about right results. (James Allen)

At the beginning of the project you probably thought about what shape your end product would take, but when exactly do you know you are done? For example, if you're creating an online tutorial for a class, when can you finish? When the website is mounted? When you've received feedback from students and incorporated their suggestions? Or will this be an ongoing project where you update the website every semester? Often completing the creation of the end product of your collaboration is not the final step of the project. You might have to create advertising for your product, test it on a sample audience, and then revise it to match the audience needs. If your group has a charge, make sure it spells out what will be expected of the group before you are finished. If not, you and your group members ought to decide on guidelines for finishing the project.

Getting support

> One of the worst things you can do is have a limited budget and try to do some big looking film. That's when you end up with very bad work. (Roger Corman)

Collaborations can only succeed if group members get support – both time and resources – from their institutions. If you are a supervisor, reward collaboration by allowing time off for your staff to work on group projects. Try to marshal technology resources which may be necessary for the project's success. Realise the importance of collaboration when creating a budget to fund staff professional development. If you are a collaborative group member, promote collaborations to your manager. Encourage your supervisor to give you the time or scheduling flexibility necessary to participate in the collaboration. Let them know that collaborations are often the best approach to solving problems shared by departments, libraries, and institutions.

You might find that your project needs monetary or technological support that isn't available at your workplace. If you are working with faculty, see if their department can provide some of this support. This can also be true if you are collaborating with colleagues from other institutions. You may want to consider applying for a grant to cover the costs of your collaboration project. Many schools provide project funding to collaborations, especially those that make innovative use of technology.

Conclusion

Collaborations can meet and often exceed expectations if all the right planning is done and in place before the project begins in earnest. The most important step is to define your project clearly so that all planning then flows from that definition. In a well thought out and well planned project you will know your audience and have all the tasks defined and delegated to the right people so that you reach the end with a final product in hand. A plan will give you guidance in picking participants and knowing what technology tools and skills are necessary to make your collaboration work. However, no project can get off the ground without proper support. You may have to become an advocate for collaboration at your institution before you ever begin.

5

Evaluation: why and how

Introduction

As anyone who has studied management of any kind will know, evaluation is one of the most useful and vital parts of the management process. Evaluation is a key element in many other parts of work. Evaluation is vital to teaching, to job performance, to project management, and to self-management. Sadly, evaluation often gets left out, not only in the planning stages of work and specific projects, but also after the project is complete. Rarely do we take the time to re-group and talk, or even just think, about what happened and how it happened so that we can figure out what we learned in the process of doing and completing the work, and ask ourselves how did it go? Did we reach our goals? If we didn't, why? What would we do differently if we choose to repeat the project? What about this project is applicable to future work and/or projects? Did anything happen that we didn't expect? Was there something we expected to happen that didn't? Whew! Just a review of those questions alone can make you realise the value of evaluation.

In collaborations, evaluations are vital and integral. This is especially true for the many of us for whom collaboration is a new way of working. Thus, through evaluation we can find out how we did what we did, and whether it was worth it.

In many respects, evaluation is very similar to the initial project planning phase. You may follow many of the same routes of inquiry, but the difference is that you will be looking backwards as well as forwards. In addition, you have more people's insights and experiences to add to the inquiry, that is, all the participants and/or recipients of your collaborative project. All of these people can be asked meaningful and applicable questions about their experience of or role in the collaboration.

> As a medical doctor, it is my duty to evaluate the situation with as much data as I can gather and as much expertise as I have and as much experience as I have to determine whether or not the wish of the patient is medically justified. (Jack Kevorkian)

Formal mechanisms for evaluations

When planning your collaborations, we recommend building formal meetings into your process to gather evaluative feedback. You will want to ask yourselves how the project is going, and then plan for adjustments as needed. It is often wise, especially in new or young collaborations, not to be stringent in the project design or plan but to incorporate a testing or analysis component. This allows your team of collaborators to figure out how things did or did not work, why this was, and finally to correct for them. Then, when looking back during the evaluation phases, you can gather that information together into a usable form for when you are considering and/or planning further collaborations.

> Learn to adjust yourself to the conditions you have to endure, but make a point of trying to alter or correct

conditions so that they are most favorable to you. (William Frederick Book)

This looser style of working together and in planning overall can be antithetical to how some librarians work. This kind of organising structure can require a leap of faith for some people, while others of us are used to flying by the seats of our pants, or even winging it. Being open to differences, being willing to change, and having the overall ability to focus on flexibility are vital when thinking about the evaluation part of your collaboration. Generally speaking, the skills needed for evaluation are really not all that different from those used in the broader collaboration itself.

Stay committed to your decisions, but stay flexible in your approach. (Tony Robbins)

So, how do you make sure that the project is meeting its goals and deadlines? Well, first we have to back up and make sure you have not only set the requisite goals and deadlines, but that all the collaborators know what the deadlines and goals are. As part of the planning process, add formalised times during the project to stop, take stock of where you are, and make adjustments based on the new knowledge gained from the evaluation. You will know better how to continue in the project and how to reach your goals.

One always has time enough, if one will apply it well. (Johann Wolfgang von Goethe)

At some point in your evaluation you may find that the goals have changed, and that you have to re-evaluate your process and the project to see if you have the resources to attain the new goals. You will have to ask yourself if you have the stuff, people, and time to reach these new goals. Without this part of the evaluation you would all continue to work towards a goal or goals that are no longer applicable or even viable, thus rendering your work irrelevant and/or the goals now impossible to reach.

So, make sure to include in your Gantt chart or project plan, or list of project events, formal points of evaluation all through the process, and, perhaps as a ground rule, agree to take these moments of reflection seriously, and be willing to adjust the process as necessary.

> I can't change the direction of the wind, but I can adjust my sails to always reach my destination. (Jimmy Dean)

Some people get so wedded to the process that they lose sight of ever-shifting goals. All parties in a collaboration will need to be aware throughout the project that it's not just the *what* and *when* of the collaboration, it is also the *why* and the *how* that drive the what and when. Everyone must keep the why and how in mind.

Types of evaluation

Scheduled, regular evaluation discussions

The scheduled discussions can be a whole meeting unto themselves, or as part of another meeting. For the evaluation part, a good way to begin is with a round robin, where every member takes a turn reporting on progress for their area or part of the work, making sure they focus on progress, new information or insights, external or internal change factors, and possible applicable new technology or related projects. After each member has reported, it is a good idea for the group to review whether any of the information affects the project, the end goals, or the tasks of particular members, and then decide how to move forward by re-allocating tasks or resources as needed. The group can look over the entire project schedule and see if there are any new obstacles they will need to prepare for or accommodate in the schedule or overall plan.

> Program testing can be used to show the presence of bugs, but never to show their absence! (Edsger Dijkstra)

Feedback forms

If your collaborative project involves working with, or doing work for students, faculty or other library users, you may want to consider creating feedback forms to gather on the spot evaluation.

One standard form for instruction is the 3-2-1 form (Figure 5.1). These six questions, separated into three areas can provide a wealth of information. The first three questions let the trainer or teacher get immediate feedback on whether or not the main points of the class or session reached the audience. The instructor can self-assess whether they need to adjust what they focused on during the class and immediately make adjustments to the lecture, length of time spent on various topics, or even leave out superfluous information that the students focused on instead of the main points.

The second part with two questions helps the instructor figure out what was unclear, or left out entirely, and perhaps some insight into what the students thought they would be learning in the session.

The third part allows the student to give feedback on the teaching style of the instructor, the temperature of the room, the comfort of the chairs, or anything else they may want the instructor to know.

Figure 5.1 The 3-2-1 form

Date _____

Event or course number _____

List three things that you learned in this session.

1._____

2._____

3._____

List two things that you still don't understand.

1._____

2._____

List one thing that you would change about this session.

_____

Optional: Please send me more information about: _____

_____

Name: _____ E-mail: _____

The final part gives the students a chance to ask for immediate feedback on a specific question, in case they had to leave for another class immediately, they think their question is slightly off topic, or perhaps they are just shy or think their question may be stupid. Some people feel more comfortable writing them down and handing them to you so you can get back to them later.

A note here: in order for these evaluations to be helpful, the feedback must be taken into account and taken seriously by the instructor or presenter. Perhaps the feedback is unexpected, or perhaps something you don't want to hear. You owe yourself and the collaboration the courtesy of taking these seriously. Take the time to consider the feedback and work towards incorporating what you have learned into your project or activity the next time you offer the same type of event or class. Indeed, one of the authors keeps the filled out forms handy and reviews them before beginning a similar project. Sometimes the time between sessions can be a semester or a year, and you can use these to refresh your memory of how it went last time.

In addition, these types of forms are adaptable to almost any presentation or study in a library; you could modify them for usability studies, presentations or workshops in lieu of a longer evaluation form. If you aren't getting longer questionnaires back, try a shorter one modelled on this 3-2-1 form.

Surveys: paper, web and e-mail

Many books, articles and continuing education workshops are available on how to design, create and monitor surveys. In addition, there is plenty of advice out there on how to interpret the data. Below is a very brief discussion of surveys, especially including insights on what we have learned from our own surveys over the years. We have included an extensive bibliography on surveys for your further reading, study and possible use.

> Everyone takes surveys. Whoever makes a statement about human behavior has engaged in a survey of some sort. (Andrew Greeley)

Paper surveys

Paper surveys are low-tech and sometimes easier to quickly create and administer. They can be a good way to gather evaluative feedback. Researchers in the social sciences have uncovered some key elements to include in paper surveys and tips for creating and giving surveys. Some of these can also apply to web and e-mail surveys.

- *Keep your survey short.* You may want to find out lots of information from the survey respondents. Indeed, since you have their attention, the temptation will be to do just that. But here's the thing: if your survey is long, looks long (even though it might not be), or gives the impression of taking a lot of figuring out to just respond to it, very few people will actually respond. There is a balance between survey length and response. Find that balance and stick to it. Don't try to do too many things with your survey. Find the three or four things that you want to gather feedback on and stick to those. Be wary of others trying to tack more questions on to your survey, be firm and stick to your main three or four points. Stay focused and you will receive a much better response rate.

- *Put demographic questions first.* This increases the likelihood that people will take the survey. They are sucked in because they see that the answers to the first questions are easy – they know the answers. Once they have filled in the first few blanks for name, date, etc., they have already made a commitment to the survey and are more likely to finish it.

- *Make sure the questions you ask will gather the kind of information you need.* Attitudes, behaviour, knowledge, and participant demographics affect how you write your survey questions. Measure attitude with questions that ask respondents how they feel. Behaviour questions ask respondents what they do. Especially, remember to ask about short time spans to get more precise answers. Knowledge questions are not used very often but they can identify gaps in what respondents know. For demographic questions, it is important to make sure these types of questions are relevant to the survey and the targeted respondents.

- *Be clear in the survey instructions.* Use language that is equivalent to what is asked for in the survey. For example, when asking them to check in boxes next to their answers, make sure there are boxes for them to check. Have the survey copy edited.

- *Thank them for taking the time to respond.* This can be done at the beginning or the end of the survey instrument or form.

- *Test your survey exhaustively.* Make sure you have lots of different kinds of people test your survey, then use their feedback to change it. It is important to keep an open mind – if someone suggests that you change something that you are sure cannot be correct, it is probably time to pull back and trust them. You are too close to the survey to look at it objectively – remember, the whole point of testing and gathering feedback is to go beyond your own narrow view to see how others respond.

- *Look into any use of human subjects requirements at your institution.* In the USA, the federal government has become more stringent in the past decade, and you may have to make sure your survey fits the requirements of your institution's board. This will most likely vary from country to country, but it is a good idea to do what you need to early on, so that your project can proceed in a timely manner.

- *Offer incentives.* For really short surveys you may not need to offer incentives, but if you are asking for feedback on a longer survey, then offer some kind of incentive. Sometimes this can just be assurance that you will make the results of the survey publicly available, assuring them that individual responses are confidential.

Web surveys

Many types of software packages offer some sort of web survey building tool. There are probably some available to you at your institution or university. Many of these survey building tools are part of web management software, or sometimes even part of the e-mail software. Ask your systems department or technology people if they know whether your institution already owns any software packages that have survey creation capability, and that may already be available to you. In our experience, many systems staff have either played around with the survey software, or even used it. They can be good resources and collaborators in creating your web survey.

Another option is free web survey software. Some companies offer access to free survey building tools, and, for a few reasons, these may be a good thing to use the first time you offer a survey. First, you may not have access to the money to buy the software. Second, you can try out the software without an outlay of money, and perhaps, after you have shown the results and usefulness of your survey, make a case for your institution to invest in survey software. A Google search for 'web survey software' brings up links to a huge variety of companies offering such software.

We picked a company at random to review in more detail. The company, WebSurveyor, offers a few free tools to create questionnaires. In addition, they also offer options for purchase. There are many software options out there to use to create and administer web surveys. Before you purchase any software, make sure you understand how the data are gathered, compiled and presented, as it is very important to have the ability to manipulate the data for reports after the survey has been conducted. You will want to be able to export the data, and easily transform it into various formats, for reports or discussion. There are usually ratings and recommendations on various products also available on the Web which you will probably want to read before you buy or write up a proposal to secure funding.

While many of the key elements and tips are the same for web surveys as for paper surveys, there are some that are particular to web surveys.

- *As with paper surveys, pre-testing is vital to giving a web survey.* It is particularly important for web surveys to be tested out using different platforms, browsers, Internet connections, etc. You will want to make sure that there are no impediments to possible respondents gaining access to and successfully submitting their surveys. If your survey will only work in one or more specific browsers, make sure you mention this in your survey instructions. You want to make sure that your survey is not confusing to anyone.

- *Include testing of survey data manipulation.* It is tragic indeed to conduct a survey and then find out after you have gathered all the data, that the software you used won't let you easily use or manipulate the data. Find out if multiple people can easily access the results. This could be an issue if the members of your collaboration team are not in close proximity to one another. If everyone can access the data, then that is one less task to assign to a collaboration team member. Again, pay close attention to how the software displays and exports the data.

- *Include an option for respondents to respond in print.* They will need to be able to print the survey form, manually complete it with pen or pencil, and then mail the completed form to you. Some people will not feel comfortable with any part of taking a web survey, such as the actual manipulation of a web form. Concerns about security and confidentiality can keep some people from filling out a survey. Giving multiple options for responding can help with securing more respondents.

E-mail surveys

The key to e-mail surveys, more than surveys in any other format, is that they must be brief. For a survey sent and responded to via e-mail, the length should be no more than one screen, at best. Given the nature of e-mails and the large number that many of us now receive and respond to on a daily basis, asking people to respond to a lengthy e-mail survey is asking too much. If, however, it is a brief survey – two to four questions at most – then e-mail is appropriate.

In conclusion, surveys can be powerful tools for gathering evaluative feedback for collaborations. One skill of a collaborator could be their previous experience in surveys or evaluations. However, through doing it yourself the first time around, you will gain valuable experience that you can use for future collaborations, as well as in other parts of your job.

> Therefore, let us not despair, but instead, survey the position, consider carefully the action we must take, and then address ourselves to our common task in a mood of sober resolution and quiet confidence, without haste and without pause. (Arthur Henderson)

Conclusion

In conclusion, evaluation is a vital part of any undertaking. We must evaluate what may affect our project at the outset of the work. To evaluate ourselves and our work as we go along will keep us on track. And after our work is done, we owe it to ourselves to figure out, through evaluation, what went well, and what didn't. Many never learn from their mistakes because they do not take the time to evaluate. Don't let that be you.

Further reading

Ashmore, B. and Morris, S. E. (2002) 'From scraps to reams: a survey of printing services in academic libraries'. *College & Research Libraries* 63(4): 342–52.

Banks, J. (1996) 'Student use of a reserve collection: a survey'. *Collection Building* 15(2): 31–5.

Bar-Ilan, J., Peritz, B. C. and Wolman Y. (2003) 'A survey on the use of electronic databases and electronic journals accessed through the web by the academic staff of Israeli universities'. *The Journal of Academic Librarianship* 29(6): 346–61.

Barksdale-Hall, R. C. (2002) 'Navigating the new leadership frontier: African American librarians and service in the 21st century: survey results'. *Urban Library Journal* 11(2): 47–60.

Baron, S. and Strout-Dapaz, A. C. (2001) 'Communicating with and empowering international students with a library skills set: survey of academic libraries belonging to Texshare and Amigos'. *Reference Services Review* 29(4): 314–26.

Bazirjian, R. (2004). 'The administration and management of integrated library systems: a survey and results'. *Library Resources & Technical Services* 48(1): 34–47.

Benefiel, C. R. and Smith, S. (1991) 'Firstsearch: a survey of end-users'. *OCLC Systems & Services* 7(6): 16–18.

Boydston, J. M. K. and Leysen J. M. (2002). 'Internet resources cataloging in ARL libraries: staffing and access issues: survey results'. *The Serials Librarian* 41(3/4): 127–45.

Brinkman, C. S., Kulkarni J. M. and Lavallee-Welch, C. (2002) 'User input into the planning of a computer lab within a library: a survey of faculty and students at the Laura Kersey Library'. *Kentucky Libraries* 66(4): 26–30.

Burkell, J. (2003) 'The dilemma of survey nonresponse'. *Library & Information Science Research* 25(3): 239–63.

Calvert, P. and Pope A. (2005) 'Telephone survey research for library managers'. *Library Management* 26(3): 139–51.

Chase, R. L. (1997) 'The knowledge-based organization: an international survey'. *Journal of Knowledge Management* 1(1): 38–49.

Clayden, J. (2002) 'Out in the wide world with a new "piece of paper": a survey of graduates of Edith Cowan University's Bachelor of Science (Library Technology)'. *Australian Library Journal* 51(2): 143–55.

Cork, S. A. (2002) 'Membership in MLA: A survey of USM library and information science students'. *Mississippi Libraries* 66(4): 113–14.

Courtney, N. (2003) 'Unaffiliated users access to academic libraries: a survey'. *The Journal of Academic Librarianship* 29(1): 3–7.

Cox, J. (2003) 'Value for money in electronic journals: a survey of the early evidence and some preliminary conclusions'. *Serials Review* 29(2): 83–8.

Craig, S. (2003) 'Survey of current practices in art and architecture libraries'. *Journal of Library Administration* 39(1): 91–107.

Cranford, J. L. (2002) *Survey on Food and Drink in Law Libraries.* Buffalo, NY: WS Hein & Co.

Curtis, S. C. and Mann, B. J. (2002). 'Cooperative reference: is there a consortium model? Survey results'. *Reference & User Services Quarterly* 41(4): 344–9.

Dalrymple, C. (2002). 'Perceptions and practices of learning styles in library instruction. survey of members of ALA library instruction round table'. *College & Research Libraries* 63(3): 261–73.

Despines, J. (2001) 'Planning for extended hours: a survey of practice'. *Knowledge Quest* 30(2): 22–6.

Dillon, I. F. and Hahn K. L. (2002) 'Are researchers ready for the electronic-only journal collections? Results of a survey at the University of Maryland'. *Portal* 2(3): 375–90.

Dinerman, G. (2002) 'If you don't know, ask: the art and craft of survey'. *Information Outlook* 6(7): 6–10.

Dong, X. (2003) 'Searching information and evaluation of internet: a Chinese academic user survey'. *International Information & Library Review* 35(2/4): 163–87.

Duranceau, E. F. and Hepfer, C. (2002). 'Staffing for electronic resource management: the results of a survey'. *Serials Review* 28(4): 316–20.

East, J. W. (2003) 'Australian library resources in philosophy: a survey of recent monograph holdings'. *Australian Academic & Research Libraries* 34(2): 92–9.

Epstein, J. and Klinkenberg, W. D. (2002) 'Collecting data via the internet: the development and deployment of a web-based survey' in Menon, G. M (ed) *Using the Internet as a Research Tool for Social Work and Human Services*. Binghamton, NY: Haworth Press; pp. 33–47.

Francoeur, S. (2001) 'An analytical survey of chat reference services: trends and software'. *Reference Services Review* 29(3): 189–203.

Gardner, S. (2001) 'The impact of electronic journals on library staff at ARL member institutions: a survey and a critique of the survey methodology'. *Serials Review* 27(3/4): 17–32.

Gerlich, B. K. and Perrier, A. (2003) 'Arts instruction in the age of technology: providing library services to support studio and survey faculty who use technology for instruction'. *Information Technology and Libraries* 22(2): 79–83.

Glynn, T. and Wu, C. (2003) 'New roles and opportunities for academic library liaisons: a survey and recommendations'. *Reference Services Review* 31(2): 122–8.

Gonzalez, J. E. (2002) 'Present day use of the internet for survey-based research' in Menon, G. M (ed) *Using the Internet as a Research Tool for Social Work and Human Services*. Binghamton, NY: Haworth Press; pp. 19–31.

Guerrero, T. (2000) 'Libraries and nontraditional students: a brief survey of contemporary services and programs'. *Current Studies in Librarianship* 24(1/2): 93–106.

Hackenberg, J. M. and Chu, B. (2002) 'Why does one choose sci-tech librarianship? Findings of a survey'. *Science & Technology Libraries* 23(1): 3–16.

He, S. (2003) 'Informatics: a brief survey'. *The Electronic Library* 21(2): 117–22.

Hemmens, A. E. (2002) 'Advanced legal research courses: a survey of ABA-accredited law schools'. *Law Library Journal* 94(2): 209–41.

Institute of Library and Museum Services. (2004) 'The institute to survey training programs for library staff'. *Library Mosaics* 15(4): 19.

Jackson, P. A. (2005) 'Incoming international students and the library: a survey'. *Reference Services Review* 33(2): 197–209.

Janes, J. (1999) 'Survey construction'. *Library Hi Tech* 17(3): 321–25.

Janes, J. (2001) 'Survey research design'. *Library Hi Tech* 19(4): 419–21.

Janes, J. (2002) 'Digital reference: reference librarians' experiences and attitudes: survey of librarians in public and academic libraries'. *Journal of the American Society for Information Science and Technology* 53(7): 549–66.

Johnson, K. and Fountain, K. C. (2002) 'Laying a foundation for comparing departmental structures between reference and instructional services: analysis of a nationwide survey'. *College & Research Libraries* 63(3): 275–87.

Justiss, L. (2003) 'A survey of fee-based web subscriptions in academic law libraries'. *Law Library Journal* 95(3): 383–409.

Keller, A. (2001) 'Future development of electronic journals: a Delphi survey'. *The Electronic Library* 19(6): 383–96.

Kelley, K. B. and Orr, G. J. (2003) 'Trends in distant student use of electronic resources: a survey'. *College & Research Libraries* 64(3): 176–91.

Kemoni, H. N. (2002) 'The utilisation of archival information by researchers in Kenya: a case study of the University of Nairobi: survey among University of Nairobi faculty about their use of the national archives and documentation service'. *African Journal of Library, Archives & Information Science* 12(1): 69–80.

Klarin, S., Pigac, S. and Pavelic, D. (2001) 'Croatian remote access electronic serials: results of a survey'. *International Cataloguing and Bibliographic Control* 30(4): 70–2.

Koteles, C. and Haythornthwaite, C. (2002) 'Undergraduate programs in information science: a survey of requirements and goals'. *Journal of Education for Library and Information Science* 43(2): 144–54.

Lee, D. (2004) 'Marketing research: survey basics'. *Library Administration & Management* 18(2): 98–9.

Lee, W. M. and Sinn R. N. (2002) 'Scientists and the journal article: choices for access: survey on document delivery preferences at the University of Toledo'. *Journal of Interlibrary Loan, Document Delivery & Information Supply* 12(3): 37–56.

Love, J. B. (2002) 'The enhanced and changing role of the specialist librarian: survey of education librarians'. *The Reference Librarian* 78: 149–65.

Lumande, E. and Mutshewa, A. (2002). 'The Botswana Library Association: attitudes to membership among librarians in Botswana: survey results'. *Information Development* 18(2): 117–25.

Manjunatha, K. and Shivalingaiah, D. (2001) 'Marketing of library and information services; a study of attitude of librarians: survey of librarians in India'. *Herald of Library Science* 40(3/4): 172–85.

Miller, J. M. (2004) 'Issues surrounding the administration of a credit course for medical students: survey of US academic health sciences librarians'. *Journal of the Medical Library Association* 92(3): 354–63.

Murgai, S. R. (2002) 'When library surveys result in positive action: a success story (a report of a library survey at the University of Tennessee/Chattanooga)'. *Tennessee Librarian* 53(1): 5–23.

Murray, P. E. (2001) 'Library web proxy use survey results'. *Information Technology and Libraries* 20(4): 172–8.

Oladokun, O. S. and Fidzani, B. T. (2002) 'The provision of library support service in colleges of education in Botswana: survey of six libraries'. *African Journal of Library, Archives & Information Science* 12(1): 47–57.

Owen, D. J. and Fang, M.-L. E. (2003) 'Information-seeking behavior in complementary and alternative medicine (CAM): an online survey of faculty at a health sciences campus'. *Journal of the Medical Library Association* 91(3): 311–21.

Porter, D. C. (2002) 'Medievalists' use of electronic resources: the results of a national survey of faculty members in medieval studies'. Thesis MSLS. University of North Carolina at Chapel Hill.

Powell, C. A. and Case-Smith, J. (2003). 'Information literacy skills of occupational therapy graduates: a survey of learning outcomes'. *Journal of the Medical Library Association* 91(4): 468–77.

Rich, L. A. and Rabine, J. L. (2001). 'The changing access to electronic journals: a survey of academic library websites revisited'. *Serials Review* 27(3/4): 1–16.

Rodman, R. L. (2003) 'Cost analysis and student survey results of library support for distance education at Ohio State University'. *Journal of the Medical Library Association* 91(1): 72–8.

Row, J. S., Shrode, F. G. and Smith, R. H. (2001) 'Across the disciplines: does subsidized document delivery meet the challenges? User survey at the University of Tennessee, Knoxville'. *Collection Management* 26(2): 13–29.

Sauer, C. K. (2001) 'Doing the best we can? The use of collection development policies and cooperative collecting activities at manuscript repositories: survey of US repositories'. *The American Archivist* 64(2): 308–49.

Sayed, E. N. and Murray, S. D. (2003) 'User satisfaction survey and usage of an electronic desktop document delivery service at an academic medical library'. *Medical Reference Services Quarterly* 22(4): 21–9.

Smith, K. J. (2002) 'Professor attendance as a factor in perceived library instruction effectiveness: an exploratory study: survey of instruction librarians'. *Reference Services Review* 30(1): 43–8.

Su, S.-F. (2001) 'Attitudes toward scholarly electronic journals: quantitative survey results in Europe and North America' [Text in Chinese]. *Journal of Educational Media & Library Sciences* 39(2): 131–44.

Tag, S. G. (2004) 'A library instruction survey for transfer students: implications for library services'. *The Journal of Academic Librarianship* 30(2): 102–8.

Tenopir, C and Ennis, L. A. (2002) 'A decade of digital reference: 1991–2001: survey results from ARL libraries'. *Reference & User Services Quarterly* 41(3): 264–73.

Tillotson, J, (2002) 'Website evaluation: a survey of undergraduates'. *Online Information Review* 26(6): 392–403.

Turpening, P. K. (2002) 'Survey of preservation efforts in law libraries'. *Law Library Journal* 94(3): 363–93.

Tyler, A. (2001) 'A survey of distance learning library and information science courses delivered via the internet'. *Education for Information* 19(1): 47–59.

Ward, M. L. (2001) 'A survey of engineers in their information world: principal engineers at Ricardo Consulting Engineers'. *Journal of Librarianship and Information Science* 33(4): 168–76.

Ward, R., Michaelis, D. and Murdoch, R. (2003) 'Widespread academic efforts address the scholarly communication crisis: the results of a survey of academic institutions'. *College & Research Libraries News* 64(6): 382–3, 89.

Wells, K. L. (2004) 'Hard times in technical services: how do academic libraries manage? A survey'. *Technical Services Quarterly* 21(4): 17–30.

Young, H. (2002). 'Law librarians' survey: are academic law librarians in decline?' *Legal Information Management* 2(2): 50–5.

6

Peer collaboration

Overview

The cases in this chapter focus on peer collaboration, whether internal or external. By peer collaboration we mean the collaborators are all librarians who have similar job titles or responsibilities, be they from the same library, same library system, or similar librarians who work for different universities.

These peer collaborations offer the least number of challenges to collaborating because the participants often have more in common than with members of other types of collaborations. The biggest challenges to peer collaboration will be in overcoming differences in work styles and work schedules. There may also be differences to overcome with the cultures of departments, libraries or institutions. Later chapters will have case studies that cover collaborations with external participants who have very different job titles and/or responsibilities.

These case studies focus primarily on instruction, because it lends itself well to collaboration, especially peer collaboration. Through peer collaborations we can share the instruction design, the actual teaching – especially by bringing each of the partners' strengths to the table. In many cases we can also share resources and handouts, so that we don't have to keep reinventing the wheel every time we have to teach an instruction session.

We know many of you are already teaching and team-teaching, so we hope these case studies will give you new ideas for your own collaborations. As with any collaboration, if you find your collaborations turning sour, turn back to the first part of this book, and use some of the tools and tips to see if you can improve your collaboration the next time around. Don't give up! We have found that many collaborations can start out slow, or on the wrong foot, but can be brought back on track with some re-adjustments.

At the end of this chapter is a list of articles from the past 15 years where many librarians have written about their own peer collaborations, especially in offering instruction.

Team teaching

- *Participants*: instruction librarians and subject librarians who teach.

- *Institutions/departments/others involved*: multiple departments and libraries within one library system.

- *Type of collaboration*: preparing bibliographic instruction sessions that are taught by two or more librarians.

- *Length of collaboration*: one semester plus two weeks of pre-semester planning.

- *Advantages*: leveraging the expertise and insight of multiple instruction librarians.

- *Outcomes*: bibliographic instruction sessions that are more interesting and interactive, and learning opportunities for all librarians involved.

Case narrative

Three librarians, Jane, Henry and Valissa, are all members of the John Doe Library system's team of instructors, yet instruction is just one small part of each of their job responsibilities. Jane and Valissa are both heads of branch libraries, while Henry is a subject specialist and a member of the main library's reference department. At John Doe, instruction is decentralised, and in many ways just getting off the ground, especially in curriculum integration. Henry and Valissa are both seasoned instructors, while Jane, who is new to the university, is just starting out as a teacher of bibliographic instruction. She does, however, have lots of subject expertise and is very comfortable with public speaking.

Jane decides to approach Henry and Valissa and ask if they would be willing to team teach with her for her first forays into library instruction. She has heard through the grapevine that they are both excellent instructors and both of them seem approachable. Jane sends them e-mail to ask, as she has not done much instruction, would either or both of them would be willing to team up with her to teach the bibliographic sessions she has signed up to give in the fall semester. Both Henry and Valissa readily agree and suggest that they all meet for a lunch meeting in the next few days.

At Jane's meeting later that same day with her boss, the director of library public services, she tells him that she has signed up to teach a few bibliographic instruction sessions in the coming semester, and that she has contacted Henry and Valissa to team teach with her. The director tells Jane that he is glad she is getting started on learning a new skill, and that Valissa and Henry are terrific teachers as well as good collaboration partners. He encourages her to learn all she can from them and that if she needs any help from him, he will be glad to do so.

During their lunch meeting two days later, Jane confesses that she is a little nervous about teaching, and team teaching right away feels like a daunting task. Valissa suggests that Jane observe a few sessions of other instructors before she takes on the task. Jane agrees, but thinks they could go ahead and plan out their own sessions at lunch, at least discuss what topics Henry and Valissa know will need to be covered in the bibliographic instructions sessions. By the end of the lunch, the partners have set up two more working lunches and Jane has a list of librarians to contact to ask about observing. The three of them have also split up the databases they want to cover in their own session, so that each of them will be responsible for knowing at least one resource really well. Henry has agreed to contact by e-mail the professor who Jane has signed up for, making sure that he will copy the message to Jane so she can read how Henry approaches professors beforehand. Jane walks back to her library feeling that learning bibliographic instruction won't be as difficult as she imagined.

The day for her first observation rolls around and Jane arrives early to the library training room. She introduces herself to the librarian who will be conducting the bibliographic instruction session and then sits in the back to observe. She takes lots of notes and pays close attention to the teaching techniques of the librarian. When she gets back to her office afterwards, she phones Valissa to debrief her on the session. She learned a good technique to evaluate whether or not the students had paid attention during the session and/or understood what was important in the class. Valissa agrees that this student evaluation sounds like it would work and invites Jane to observe her own session the next day.

After a few more observation sessions Jane feels ready to team teach. She knows she is not ready to go it alone, but with Henry or Valissa she knows she could handle at least a third or a half of an instruction session. So she e-mails them to let them know, and includes in the e-mail her ideas for how she plans to teach her database to the class. Henry e-mails back and gives her a few more ideas on what to include and says the professor would like to have the first session next week.

The first class goes without any problems. Because Henry, Jane and Valissa are prepared, they are able to skip over parts of the topics they want to cover because the students say they already know how to use that resource. When, near the end of the session, one of the students asks how to find a book in the law library, Jane pipes up with a good description of how to do it.

In their debriefing session on the walk back to the main campus, Jane and her two team members talk about how the session went. Jane says she appreciated it when Henry fielded a question during her section because she did not know the answer off the top of her head. Valissa points out that Jane would probably want to walk around more when she was introducing herself and the other trainers so that the students don't get bored right at the beginning of the session. Henry comments that he really liked the evaluation technique Jane had the students do at the end of the session – it really accomplished multiple things, especially reiterating for the students in their own words the main points of the demonstration. All agree that they are looking forward to the next session they will team teach the next week.

Questions

1. What were some of the attributes of the collaborators that made this session work?

2. What planning and evaluation techniques did they use?

3. What did each of the collaborators learn from the experience?

Writing a book

- *Collaborators*: Teddy, KT and Anne (nope, we didn't change our names for this one!)

- *Institutions/departments/others involved*: one state and one private university.

- *Type of collaboration*: joint writing of a book.

- *Length of collaboration*: six months: planning – two months, writing, revising, and final edit – four months.

- *Advantages to collaboration*: previous working relationships, similar working styles, ability to use track changes to edit work, no big egos, willingness to do the writing.

- *Disadvantages*: two of the partners (KT and Teddy) had never met in person.

- *Outcomes*: a published book, and the impetus to work together again and write another one.

Case narrative

Anne had really wanted to write a book on how librarians can function better in their role with the library as an institution. When she saw an e-mail from a publisher soliciting ideas for books in library and information science, she thought why not submit one. She also thought, as she didn't want to write the whole thing by herself, and if she could get a deal from the publisher, why not invite two younger librarians she was informally mentoring to be co-authors with her. So she asked KT and Teddy, both of whom readily agreed. They submitted the jointly written proposal via e-mail to the publisher, with Anne serving as the main author. The proposal was accepted and a due date was negotiated with the publisher and between the partners, and the planning began.

E-mails flew back and forth with initial proposals for timeline, editing schedule, writing time, etc. proposed by any of the partners and then revised by any of the partners. A date was set for the first drafts to be completed. They all thought that sounded feasible. KT, Teddy and Anne were left to their own devices to write the initial drafts.

The due date arrived and each of the authors had indeed written first drafts of their assigned chapters. These they sent via e-mail to each other. KT suggested that they use the track changes option in Microsoft Word, and that after an edit was complete, the editor rename the file (e.g. 'KT's Edit of Chapter 2'). Afterwards, all would send the edits to the chapter's original author, who would then be in charge of the final editing. As they worked through the process they made a few changes in the way they named the files they exchanged, as some chapters went into second and third revisions – KT solved these issues by suggesting that they change the colour of the fonts in the later versions.

For the final month before the due date, the e-mails were coming and going fast and furiously. Teddy and Anne decided that the chapters would work better if applicable quotes were added in, so they split up the chapters, and each searched for and inserted quotes as necessary. They alerted KT to what they were doing, and she thought that was a terrific idea, but as a project had come up at her library, she could not help them in the final preparations stages. Neither Anne nor Teddy minded, so they jumped back into their search for quotes.

Once the book was sent off, they all three breathed a collective sigh of relief. A month or so later, the publisher e-mailed them and asked if they would be willing to create an index to the book. KT proposed a method of how to approach this, and all three jumped in to complete the index in the time they were given. That too was sent off to the publisher. More collective sighs of relief were heard.

The book was published, and occasionally one of the partners would search for their title on the database WorldCat, an online union catalogue, to see how many libraries worldwide had catalogued the book, and then share that number with the other partners. Finally, after the book had been out for a while, and they received their first royalty cheque, the time had come for Teddy and KT to meet in person. So Anne and Teddy travelled to a restaurant near the library where KT worked and they all had pizza together and talked about possibly writing another book together. They paid for the lunch bill out of their royalties.

Questions

1. What were the attributes of the collaborators that made this collaboration work?

2. How did they use technology to help with their project?

3. What other things did they gain, besides having written a book?

Further reading

Barton, J. A. (2003) 'Promoting information literacy: an evaluation of the library's collaboration with the first-year English program at UNC-Chapel Hill'. Thesis MSLS. University of North Carolina at Chapel Hill.

Bell, C. (2002) 'Expanded conversations: collaborating for student learning: Introduction to the Special Loex-of-the-West 2002 Issue'. *Reference Services Review* 30(4): 267–68.

Black, C., Crest, S. and Volland, M. (2001) 'Building a successful information literacy infrastructure on the foundation of librarian-faculty collaboration at Towson University'. *Research Strategies* 18(3): 215–25.

Boisselle, J. H., Fliss, S. and Mestre, L. S. (2004) 'Talking toward techno-pedagogy: IT and librarian collaboration-rethinking our roles'. *Resource Sharing and Information Networks* 17(1/2): 123–6.

Bowden, T. S. and DiBenedetto, A. (2001) 'Information literacy in a biology laboratory session: an example of librarian-faculty collaboration'. *Research Strategies* 18(2): 143–9.

Boyle, F. and Clarke, L. (2003) 'Electronic resource training: subject-based collaboration'. *Library & Information Update* 2(8): 54–5.

Burggraff, D. and Kraljic, M. (2002) 'Collaboration for program enrichment: exploring JSTOR and nursing'. *Journal of Library Administration* 37(1/2): 93–100.

Byrd, C. (1990) 'Lighthouses, mannequins, and pioneer women: serendipitous encounters with teaching faculty (librarian-faculty collaboration and research)'. *The Librarian in the University*. Lanham, MD: Scarecrow Press, pp. 138–46.

Cunningham, D. and Viola, D. (2002) 'Collaboration to teach graduate students how to write more effective theses'. *Journal of the Medical Library Association* 90(3): 331–4.

D'Angelo, B. J. (2003) 'If they build it will they come? Cooperation and collaboration to create a customized library'. *The Reference Librarian* (83/84): 237–50.

Elliot, P. and Spitzer, A. M. (1999) 'Lessons of a decade: an instructional experiment matures. curriculum collaboration at Washington State University'. *The Reference Librarian* 64: 53–66.

Fain, M., Bates, P. and Stevens, R. (2003) 'Promoting collaboration with faculty'. In *Integrating Information Literacy into the College Experience*. Ann Arbor MI: Pierian Press.

Fenske, R. F. (1998) 'Computer literacy and the library: a new connection'. *Reference Services Review* 26(2): 67–72.

Fiegen, A. M., Cherry, B. and Watson, K. (2002) 'Reflections on collaboration: learning outcomes and information literacy assessment in the business curriculum at California State University, San Marcos'. *Reference Services Review* 30(4): 307–18.

Giles, K. L. (2004) 'Reflections on a privilege: becoming part of the course through a collaboration on Blackboard'. *College & Research Libraries News* 65(5): 261–3, 68.

Huber, K. and Sherman, B. (1992) 'Scholarly networking in action: faculty/librarian collaboration in teaching psychology at St. Olaf College'. *Research Strategies* 10: 40–3.

Huston, M. M. (1994) 'Instructional responses to the presence and potential of diversity: toward expert collaboration'. *The Reference Librarian* 45/46: 79–92.

Jesudason, M. (2000) 'Outreach to student-athletes through e-mail reference service'. *Reference Services Review* 28(3): 262–8.

Johnson, A. M. (2003) 'Library Instruction and information literacy'. *Reference Services Review* 31(4): 385–418.

Johnson, A. M. and Jent, S. (2004) 'Library instruction and information literacy – 2003'. *Reference Services Review* 32(4): 413–42.

Johnson, A. M. and Rader, H. B. (2002) 'Library instruction and information literacy – 2001'. *Reference Services Review* 30(4): 359–89.

Kalin, S. G. W. (2004) 'Collaboration: a key to internet training at Pennsylvania State University'. *Bulletin of the American Society for Information Science* 20: 20–1.

Lipman, C. and King-Blandford M. A. (1997) 'Innovation and collaboration brings forth a new approach to bibliographic instruction – teach the teachers. Program at the University of Toledo's Carlson Library'. *Journal of Interlibrary Loan, Document Delivery & Information Supply* 8(2): 21–31.

Lockerby, R., Lynch, D. and Sherman J. (2004) 'Collaboration and information literacy: challenges of meeting standards when working with remote faculty'. *Journal of Library Administration* 41(1/2): 243–53.

Lowe, S. S. (1995) 'Collaboration with faculty: integrating information literacy into the curriculum (at the University of Maine at Augusta)'. *Off-campus Library Services Conference*

(7th:1995:San Diego, Calif.) The Seventh Off-campus Library Services Conference Proceedings. Central Michigan University. pp. 257–60.

Macklin, A. and Fosmire, M. (2003) 'Real-world solutions for real-world collaboration problems'. In Nims, J. K., Baier, R., Bullard, R. and Owen, R. (eds) *Integrating Information Literacy into the College Experience.* Ann Arbor, MI: Pierian Press.

McCarthy, P. J. (2002) 'Instruction collaboration: imperative or imperilment?' *Colorado Libraries* 28(2): 34–5.

McCleskey, S. E. and Allison, D. J. (2000) 'Collaboration for service learning in architectural education'. *Art Documentation* 19(1): 40–3.

McMillen, P. S., Miyagishima, B. and Maughan, L. S. (2002) 'Lessons learned about developing and coordinating an instruction program with freshman composition'. *Reference Services Review* 30(4): 288–99.

Naslund, J.-A., Asselin, M. and Filipenko, M. (2005) 'Blueprint for collaboration: an information literacy project at the University of British Columbia'. *PNLA Quarterly* 69(3): 10, 29–32.

Nugent, C, R. (1998) 'Internet training through collaboration: the practicum that made a difference at Maryville College in Tennessee'. *College & Undergraduate Libraries* 5(1): 15–26.

Orians, C. and Sabol L. (1999) 'Using the web to teach library research skills in introductory biology: a collaboration between faculty and librarians'. *Issues in Science & Technology Librarianship* 23; available at *http://www.istl.org/99-summer/article2.html* (accessed: 28 October 2005).

Paglia, A. and Donahue, A. (2003) 'Collaboration works: integrating information competencies into the psychology curricula'. *Reference Services Review* 31(4): 320–8.

Petrowski, M. J., Baird, D. and Leach, K. (2000) 'Building a successful collaboration: Colgate University's collaboration for enhanced learning: faculty-librarian collaboration'. *College & Research Libraries News* 61(11): 1003–5.

Rader, H. B. (1999) 'Faculty-librarian collaboration in building the curriculum for the millennium: The US experience. Presented at the 1998 IFLA Conference'. *IFLA Journal* 25(4): 209–13.

Riedel, T. (2003) 'Added value, multiple choices: librarian/faculty collaboration in online course development'. *Journal of Library Administration* 37(3/4): 477–87.

Sauer, J. A. (1995) 'Conversation 101: process, development, and collaboration'. *Information for a New Age*. Westport, CT: Libraries Unlimited; pp. 135–51.

Scales, J., Matthews, G. and Johnson, C. M. (2005) 'Compliance, Cooperation, Collaboration and Information Literacy'. *Journal of Academic Librarianship* 31(3): 229–35.

Schloman, B. F. and Feldmann, R. M. (1993) 'Developing information gathering skills in geology students through faculty-librarian collaboration at Kent State University'. *Science & Technology Libraries* 14: 35–47.

Shane, J. M. Y. (2004) 'Formal and informal structures for collaboration on a campus-wide information literacy program'. *Resource Sharing and Information Networks* 17(1/2): 85–110.

Smart, J. (2005) 'Consistency, context and collaboration'. *Library & Information Update* 4(1/2): 30–1.

Stamatoplos, A. and Mackoy, R. (2004) 'Collaboration in library research'. *Indiana Libraries* 23(1): 2–5.

Stein, L. L. and Lamb J. M. (1998) 'Not just another bi: faculty-librarian collaboration to guide students through the research process at the University of Delaware'. *Research Strategies* 16(1): 29–39.

Truelson, J. A. (2004) 'Partnering on virtual reference using Questionpoint: Guidelines for collaboration between academic libraries in Australia/New Zealand and the US'. *Australian Academic & Research Libraries* 35(4): 301–8.

Walter, S. (2000) 'Engelond: a model for faculty-librarian collaboration in the information age: resources for 14th-century English studies incorporates library instruction and critical thinking skills at the University of Missouri Libraries'. *Information Technology and Libraries* 19(1): 34–41.

Williamson, D. (2001) 'Library and academic collaboration: a case study in teaching media communications at Griffith University'. *Australian Academic & Research Libraries* 32(1): 53–60.

Woodard, P. (1996) 'Librarian and faculty collaboration in honors 301(88): an interdisciplinary computer applications course at Hunter College'. *Research Strategies* 14: 132–44.

7

Librarian and faculty collaboration

Overview

The cases in this chapter focus on librarian–faculty collaboration. Most librarian faculty collaborations are, like peer collaborations, centred on instruction, whether for the one-time class, or for credit course, or in creating resources for faculty to use in their courses which are created by both the faculty and librarian participants. Less often, collaborations between librarians and faculty can involve collection development, scholarly communication planning, and also library committees (e.g. library planning, search committees). While some of these types of collaborations have long histories – many have been around for years in the form of library councils – we think that they can be improved upon by applying some of the tips and techniques for collaboration we talk about in this book.

These librarian–faculty collaborations can be challenging because the participants often have less in common, beyond an interest in library affairs, and perhaps subject knowledge. Challenges to librarian–faculty collaboration can include overcoming differences in work styles, work schedules, ethics, long-term schedules, disciplines and work loads. There may also be differences to overcome with the cultures of departments, subject areas (science *vs.* social science *vs.* humanities *vs.* professional schools), libraries and schools.

These case studies cover the gamut of collaboration types and are really only limited to your imagination and willingness to take risks and be flexible. Because there are vast differences between the work of librarians and the work of faculty, these types of collaborations can be very challenging yet are often the most rewarding types of collaborations for all participants, and can be especially advantageous for the library and the departments on campus. Strong librarian–faculty collaborations can build loyalty and interest for the library and its affairs on campus, and faculty can be powerful allies when interacting with the university administration. When library administrations support and encourage librarian–faculty collaborations, they become a stronger player in the life of the university.

For many of us, librarian–faculty collaborations are the scariest collaborations to initiate and work on. As mentioned in Chapters 6 and 8, with any collaboration, if you find your collaborations turning sour, turn back to the first part of this book, and use some of the tools and tips to see if you can improve your collaboration the next time around. Don't give up! We have found that many collaborations can start out slow, or on the wrong foot, but can be brought back on track with some re-adjustments.

At the end of this chapter is a list of articles from the past 15 years where many librarians have written about their own peer collaborations, especially in offering instruction.

Credit course in information retrieval

- *Collaborators*: branch librarian and professor from the department served by the library.

- *Institutions/departments/others involved*: branch library and science department.

- *Type of collaboration*: credit course in information retrieval in a specific subject area: joint design, creation and teaching of an information retrieval course.

- *Length of collaboration*: initial planning and course design – three months. Has been taught continuously for three years.

- *Advantages to collaboration*: building on previous working relationships, well-defined strengths, willingness to jump in and do it, prepare students majoring in the subject for independent study.

- *Disadvantages*: never been done before, uncertain of support from department, uncertain of interest from students.

- *Outcomes*: a credit course that is still being offered because of high student interest.

- *Details*:
  - half-credit course;
  - based on standards set by a professional society;
  - integrated into the curriculum.

Case narrative

Phyllis, a tenured science professor, and Pete, a librarian serving her department, had been collaborating on various projects as Pete arrived at the university. One of their major first projects was the creation of a web guide called – *Science Information Retrieval: An Overview*. This web guide took standards set by the education division of the professional society – expectations for information research skills for graduates with a degree in that science – and expanded these standards into explanations of how to locate these materials locally in their own library.

Shortly after this website was created and in place, Phyllis began to think about the independent study in a lab that many students chose to undertake during their senior year. She wanted to create a course with Pete which would prepare these undergraduates for their time in a research lab. These undergraduates work alongside graduate students, post-docs, researchers and faculty, and if they had some preparation ahead of the independent study, they could begin working right away once the independent study began.

Since Pete's arrival at the library, he had been exploring new ways to offer library instruction and had been meeting and talking with Phyllis and various other faculty to try and make his bibliographic instruction as curriculum-based as possible. Their talks had come to the conclusion that there was plenty that students needed to learn, but if they couldn't use what they learned right away, they tended to forget much of it.

Phyllis approached Pete early in the spring semester with her idea for the half-credit course. The idea was that Pete would spend the one class period each week required for a half-credit course by teaching the students how to use one or two of the various resources that were already part of the website Pete and Phyllis had made. Over the semester the students would have two writing assignments: one short assignment, a library guide describing how to use a library resource; and a second larger assignment, a review paper on the topic that the student would be working on in their independent study. Over the course of the semester they would research information on their topic in the various resources and databases they were learning how to use. The last month of the course would be devoted to reviewing updated drafts of all of their papers every single week to teach the students the importance of getting feedback and the value of the editing process. Pete agreed to do it and Phyllis ran off to teach a class that started in a few minutes.

The next day Phyllis e-mailed a draft syllabus to Pete, who reviewed it and e-mailed it back with a few revisions to the order in which the resource demonstrations would be taught. He also said in the e-mail that he would begin, probably later in the semester or over the summer, creating the lectures and designing the demonstrations and handouts for each class. Phyllis dropped by Pete's office later that same day and said she would take care of running their course plan by the department, getting it accepted, getting it into the course schedule, and taking care of all the other things that have to happen in order to get a course up and running. Once all that happened, if it did get accepted, the next step would be to see if any students enrolled for the course over the summer.

By the end of the summer only one student had enrolled. Phyllis and Pete decided that as it was all a test anyway, they would go ahead and teach the one student. As the university was private, they could choose to go ahead with it. So, they taught the course to their one student and asked the student for feedback on the course at the end of the semester. The feedback was positive, and the student suggested that they offer it again the next autumn. So they did.

The second year they had two students. They again gave positive feedback and suggested that Phyllis and Pete offer it again. So they did.

The third semester that they offered the course seven students enrolled. This was exciting. The class had to be modified slightly to incorporate the increase in students. But it went well, and the feedback from the students was very positive. In the spring, at the department's undergraduate poster session for the independent study students to present what they did in their labs, the students who had taken the information retrieval course raved about how much it had helped their independent study. They felt it prepared them well for the lab work, and the professors and grad students that they had worked with had been impressed with what the students already knew at the start of the independent study. Phyllis and Pete were pleased and excited.

The next autumn seven students again signed up for the course. Then during the enrolment period for the spring semester, Phyllis got requests from students that the course be offered in the spring semester, too. After consulting with Pete, if it was possible, they offered the course in the spring and had nine students. The next autumn they had eight. The next spring nine students enrolled. At the latest semester, after the class reached it full enrolment of ten students, two more students requested to be allowed to take the course. Pete and Phyllis couldn't turn them away.

Pete and Phyllis always knew that the course design was a good one, and that even if only one student was benefiting from taking it, then teaching it was worth the effort. They found out that word of mouth was their best marketing tool, and that starting small and then growing the course gradually allowed them to evaluate often how things were going and to change or tweak the course as they went along.

During the third year, Pete began using the course management system to manage the course, as urged to do so by the university. They wanted all faculty to use the software as appropriate to each course, and Pete was ready to learn something new.

Questions

1. What were the collaborative attributes of these partners?

2. How did the collaboration change over time?

3. What would you suggest as next steps for Phyllis and Pete?

Curriculum-based assignment and instruction

- *Collaborators*: subject librarian and teaching professor.

- *Institutions/departments/others involved*: branch library and academic department.

- *Type of collaboration*: instruction and class/lab assignment – design and implementation.

- *Length of collaboration*: initial planning and course design – six months.

- *Advantages to collaboration*: decrease number of basic reference questions from general chemistry students, willingness to jump in and do it.

- *Disadvantages*: never been done before, huge number of sessions to teach, need buy-in from teaching assistants (TAs).

- *Outcomes*: students who have used library resources, especially to find physical and chemical properties for chemical compounds; better student pre-lab and lab report writing.

- *Details*:
  - 40 minute how-to demonstration of the resource tools;
  - creation of the scavenger hunt worksheet;
  - logistics of scheduling 35–45 lab sections (~540 students) into a one-week period;
  - gathered feedback from TAs on feasibility and usefulness;
  - TAs graded scavenger hunt worksheets for their sections.

- What skills did each partner bring to the collaboration?

- professor: pedagogy for general chemistry education, knowledge of the needs of general chemistry students, understanding of the applicability of the assignment to the course, control of the scheduling and syllabus of the class.

- librarian: knowledge of information resources and how to demonstrate them in an instruction section, awareness of what students found confusing in their search for information.

Case narrative

Early in the spring semester, the professor and one of her graduate student assistants approached the librarian with an idea to have some kind of library assignment for the primary introductory course taught in the department. They felt that the students needed to have a good understanding of the library and its resources in principle, but that having this knowledge would help them in the course, as well as in their later studies in the subject.

The librarian was excited, especially because she had been thinking about how to create a curriculum-based assignment for the students. She desired such a class not only to teach them about the library, but as she was the only librarian in her branch, she could not be there all the time. Nor could she spend all of her time answering reference questions, as that was just one of her job responsibilities. So she readily agreed to work with them to create a library assignment, and then conduct the bibliographic instruction sessions that went along with it.

They all agreed that over the summer they would have more time to work on the assignment, so they tabled the idea until the end of the spring semester. However, it became apparent as they started working on it a few months later, they had all been thinking about the project and had some good ideas pretty well formed.

The librarian came up with the idea of a type of scavenger hunt. Perhaps they could require the students to look for information about things they would be doing for the course already. The professor agreed and immediately came up with a draft list of what the students could look for. By this time, the research assistant had left the university, but the librarian and the professor did not see this as a setback, as they were very excited about the assignment, and felt they could continue on their own.

The librarian came up with a draft of the assignment, running it by the professor as she made changes. They communicated mostly by e-mail as the professor was off campus for much of the summer. Two weeks before the semester began the professor ran the draft assignment by a group of the teaching assistants who would be running the discussion sections and grading the assignments of the students in their sections. They suggested a few changes, and the librarian gladly incorporated them into the form. They decided on a week early in the semester to conduct the bibliographic instruction sessions, and the librarian cleared her schedule for that entire week. The professor coordinated the logistics of getting each discussion section into the library for their appointed time.

The sessions went off without a hitch. The students seemed to enjoy the assignment and became heavy library users for the rest of the semester. The multiple sessions, crammed into one week's time, was a lot of work for the librarian, but she felt that the payoff was worth it. A few weeks after the sessions, a student asked her a reference question, and the librarian said, 'Didn't you learn that in the library sessions?' The student sadly replied, 'Oh, I'm in a different class and we didn't get a library session'. So, the librarian knew that word had got out that it was a useful session, and that perhaps the concept could be expanded to other courses.

At the end of the semester, the professor took the librarian out for lunch as a thank-you, and they talked about how the experiment went from each of their perspectives. They both thought the assignment and the sessions went extremely well and had accomplished what they had hoped. They agreed that the workload for the librarian was high, and that they would do some thinking before the next autumn to see if they could decrease the total number of sessions.

Questions

1. What made these people good collaborators?

2. What were the attributes of this collaboration that made it work?

3. How could these collaborators share what they learned with others?

Further reading

Bazillion, R. J. and Braun, C. L. (2001) 'Classroom, library and campus culture in a networked environment'. *Campus-Wide Information Systems* 18(2): 61–67.

Bracke, P. J. and Dickstein, R. (2002) 'Web tutorials and scalable instruction: testing the waters'. *Reference Services Review* 30(4): 330–37.

Chu, F. T.-H. (1995) 'Collaboration in a loosely coupled system: librarian-faculty relations in collection development. Case study based on his doctoral dissertation'. *Library & Information Science Research* 17: 135–50.

Cooper, C. and Gardner, B. (2001) 'Coming full circle: a library's adventure in collaboration with teaching faculty at Eastern Kentucky University'. *Kentucky Libraries* 65(3): 23–5.

Cunningham, D. and Viola, D. (2002) 'Collaboration to teach graduate students how to write more effective theses'. *Journal of the Medical Library Association* 90(3): 331–4.

Cunningham, T. H. and Lanning S. (2002) 'New frontier trail guides: faculty-librarian collaboration on information literacy'. *Reference Services Review* 30(4): 343–48.

Dickson, V. (2004) 'Collaboration plus! The development of an information literacy and communication program'. *Australian Library Journal* 53(2): 153–60.

Dorner, J. L., Taylor S. E. and Hodson-Carlton, K. (2001) 'Faculty-librarian collaboration for nursing information literacy: a tiered approach'. *Reference Services Review* 29(2): 132–41.

Doskatsch, I. (2003) 'Perceptions and perplexities of the faculty-librarian partnership: an Australian perspective'. *Reference Services Review* 31(2): 111–21.

Drummond, R. C., Mosby, A. P. and Munroe, M. H. (1991) 'A joint venture: collaboration in collection building. Faculty-bibliographer relations at Georgia State University; Presented at the 1990 Georgia Library Association Conference'. *Collection Management* 14(1–2): 59–72.

Farber, E. (1999) 'Faculty-librarian cooperation: a personal retrospective'. *Reference Services Review* 27(3): 229–34.

Hearn, M. R. (2005) 'Embedding a librarian in the classroom: an intensive information literacy model'. *Reference Services Review* 33(2): 219–27.

Holmes, G. V. and Howson, C. K. (2000) 'Grants: interdepartmental collaboration to teach grantsmanship skills at the University of North Carolina at Greensboro'. *The Bottom Line* 13(3): 146–9.

Hooks, J. D. and Corbett, F. Jr. (2005) 'Information literacy for off-campus graduate cohorts: collaboration between a university librarian and a master's of education faculty'. *Library Review* 54(4): 245–56.

Joint, N. (2005) 'Promoting practitioner-researcher collaboration in library and information science'. *Library Review* 54(5): 289–94.

Lau, J. (2001) 'Faculty-librarian collaboration: a Mexican experience'. *Reference Services Review* 29(2): 95–105.

Leonhardt, T. W. (2003) 'Behind the scenes: working through collaboration'. *Technicalities* 23(3): 9–10.

Malenfant, C. and Demers, N. E. (2004) 'Collaboration for point-of-need library instruction'. *Reference Services Review* 32(3): 264–73.

Markgraf, J. S. (2003) 'Collaboration between distance education faculty and the library: one size does not fit all'. *Journal of Library Administration* 37(3/4): 451–64.

Paglia, A. and Donahue, A. (2003) 'Collaboration works: integrating information competencies into the psychology curricula'. *Reference Services Review* 31(4): 320–8.

Raquepau, C. A. and Richards, L. M. (2002) 'Investigating the environment: teaching and learning with undergraduates in the sciences'. *Reference Services Review* 30(4): 319–23.

Rockman, I. F. (2004) 'Continuing the connections'. *Reference Services Review* 32(4): 334–35.

Shane, J. and Bell, S. J. (2003) 'Stop sending those cards: enhancing faculty-librarian collaboration using e-selection strategies'. *College & Research Libraries News* 64(9): 606–9.

Sugarman, T. S. and Demetracopoulos, C. (2001) 'Creating a web research guide: collaboration between liaisons, faculty and students'. *Reference Services Review* 29(2): 150–7.

Thaxton, L., Faccioli, M. B. and Mosby, A. P. (2004) 'Leveraging collaboration for information literacy in psychology'. *Reference Services Review* 32(2): 185–9.

Tomczyk, C. B. (1989) 'Academic media selection: a faculty and librarian collaboration'. *Operations Handbook for the Small Academic Library Greenwood Press*. United States. 269–76.

Williams, J. and Hunt, C. C. (1998) 'Library-faculty collaboration: surveying a commuter population'. *New Library World* 99(2): 72–9.

Yi, H. (2002) 'Using the internet to teach access to Asian history resources'. *Reference Services Review* 30(1): 62–7.

Young, J. (1995) 'Faculty collaboration and academic librarians. Conclusions from a survey of faculty and administrators at four universities; Reprinted from Department Advisor Spr '92'. *Catholic Library World* 66: 16–21.

8

Internal collaboration

Overview

The cases in this chapter focus on internal collaboration. Many of you are already a part of these types of collaborations, in the form of committees, task forces or groups, and matrices. While committees have been around for ages, the increase in the number of them, their inclusion of professional, paraprofessional, and technology staff, and the rising interdepartmental nature of many of them have brought new challenges to the workplace. We think the work of these internal collaborations could improve and increase with the inclusion of collaborative techniques and a collaborative mindset.

Internal collaborations can take place at any level of the library hierarchy, but often these happen in the middle and lower brackets of the organisation chart. They often involve workflow issues, technology implementation, collection management, stack maintenance, or large-scale moves. Internal collaborations are often initiated because library administrators see that particular projects will affect multiple departments, and they want to make sure the work happens smoothly, and with lots of communication.

Challenges to internal collaborations can include overcoming differences in work styles, schedules and loads. Another particular challenge to internal collaborations is the perceived status of participants. Internal collaborators must work diligently to assure all participants that no one's voice or opinion is more equal than others.

> All animals are equal, but some animals are more equal than others. (George Orwell)

These internal collaboration case studies cover the types of collaborations we have found challenging in our own experiences. Because there are vast differences in how staff members work in the various departments of the library, these types of collaborations can be very challenging. However, if library staff can learn how to collaborate with colleagues in-house, then the entire organisation can benefit.

Again, and especially with internal collaborations as we are not used to thinking of internal work as collaborations, if you find your collaborations turning sour, turn back to the first part of this book, and use some of the tools and tips to see if you can improve your collaboration the next time around. Don't give up! We have found that many collaborations can start out slow, or on the wrong foot, but can be brought back on track with some re-adjustments.

Digital projects group

- *Participants*: director of the digitisation department, subject librarians, instructional technology specialists, collection development librarian, cataloguing librarian, special collections librarian, university archivist.

- *Institutions/departments/others involved*: academic library system.

- *Type of collaboration*: soliciting proposals for digitisation projects, creating a process for choosing which projects to carry out, choosing the projects.

- *Length of collaboration*: three months for development of the process, three months of training proposers, two months of soliciting and making decisions on which projects to undertake.

- *Advantages*: leveraging the expertise and insight from all over the library system.

- *Outcomes*: a process for choosing appropriate digitisation projects.

Case narrative

When the director of library technology left for greener pastures, the library system found itself with a fully staffed and equipped digitisation production centre, but no plan in place for soliciting, selecting, and prioritising projects. The library administration decided to create a digital projects group, with members from all over the library system to create a process to gather and choose digitisation projects, and put that process into place. It was conceived that the group would function similar to a group that had existed in the library for years, working on collection management issues, ensuring that collection decisions meshed with the mission and goals of the library. Because this model worked extremely well for the library, it was hoped that perhaps the same structure would work for building in-house created digital collections.

The first time the group met, they knew that the first order of business would be how to govern and manage their process. So the entire meeting was spent talking about and approving ground rules for their meetings and the work each would do outside of the meetings. Because there were so many people involved in the group, one of the most useful ground rules they put into place was that if members missed a meeting, they were responsible for reading the meeting notes. Additionally, if an issue was discussed and decided upon at the meeting in their absence, then they were not allowed to bring up the issue at a later meeting. Any member could raise a hand if the issue was brought up at a later meeting and simply say, 'That's decided already, read the minutes,' and the person would have to drop the issue immediately. This ground rule saved the committee hours of rehashed discussion.

The second, third, and fourth monthly meetings focused on creating a process for soliciting digital projects from library staff. The group decided to offer workshops for prospective proposers, so as to encourage proposals and to ensure that the submitted proposals had enough information for the group to make decisions. The group also worked on designing the form for proposals, and they created a process to help them make their decisions once the proposals were submitted.

The workshops were conducted by the director of the digital production centre and were offered multiple times and in various libraries across campus. All staff – not just professional staff – were encouraged to attend and to send in proposals for possible digitisation projects.

As the workshops were offered, the group continued to work on designing the decision process. As there were so many members and as the whole process would be a new one, they decided that for this first time through they would not disregard any suggested process. Being new to the game, they weren't certain what would work well. One of the members suggested using a method he had encountered in a grant funding process. They would decide on criteria, rate each project according to those criteria, and then start their discussion on those projects with the highest overall scores. As the group also wanted to give feedback to all the proposers after the decisions had been made, they designed a way to gather and sort their comments on each individual project. One member who was skilled in using spreadsheet software offered to design a form for the rating of projects, as well as a word processing form for the comments.

The special collections librarian and the director of the digital processing centre came up with the idea of a project 'show and tell' for the group. This was scheduled for after the proposals had been submitted, but before the individual members had to rate each proposal. As many of the members of the group were not familiar with the materials suggested for each project, this 'show and tell' (without the presence of the proposers) ended up being a very valuable resource in the decision-making process of all of the members of the group.

Ten proposals were submitted from all parts of the library system. The group met and ranked the projects by using the ratings and the comments, as well as feasibility reports on each project created by the staff of the digital processing centre. The top four rated projects, pre-discussion, were the exact four the digital production centre staff had said were feasible for the next nine months. The committee still discussed every project at length; they also talked a little about how the process worked for each of them.

The digital production centre staff are very pleased to have projects to work on that are tied to the mission and goals of the library. The group is ready to have the first post-decision meeting to debrief, and plan for the next round of proposals, to happen in the next nine months.

Questions

1. Why was it important to have so many members on this group?

2. What do you think the reaction of the rest of the library staff will be after the projects are completed?

3. Do you think others will want to serve on the committee as members rotate off?

Library party planning group

- *Participants*: one reference librarian, one branch librarian, two paraprofessionals from the acquisitions department, two from the circulation department, and one staff assistant from the library human resources (HR) department.

- *Institutions/departments/others involved*: academic library system.

- *Type of collaboration*: planning for and giving parties for staff appreciation, in particular a summer picnic.

- *Length of collaboration*: each member serves at least one year.

- *Advantages*: leveraging the interest and party-planning expertise from all over the library system.

- *Outcomes*: a terrific party.

Case narrative

This year the party committee wanted to throw a summer picnic party that would be well remembered by as many staff as possible throughout the library system. In the past, those working on this group had heard complaints about the various functions they had offered, and they wanted to change that. Towards that end, they decided to send out a simple survey to all the staff to find out what would be the event that would make just about everyone rave. The group met to talk about what to include on the survey, and they decided to base their questions on the types of complaints that each had heard in the past.

The next step involved contacting someone from the library technology department to assist them in using the web survey software to conduct their survey. Technology staff always like a good party and were glad to help out. Once the survey was ready to go, the committee sent out an e-mail to all staff, asking for feedback on how to make the summer picnic the best ever. They got a return rate of 85 per cent so they surmised two things: people liked parties and they had strong opinions on how the parties ought to be organised. No surprise there! They also figured they were already on the right track, as they had included all of the staff in the initial planning process.

Through the survey results the group discovered that there were more vegetarians than they had originally thought (and had planned for in the past); that non-vegetarians often liked to eat the vegetarian option (which made the complaints about the vegetarian food going quickly more understandable); that almost all respondents wanted shared group activities; that the event needed to happen during work hours; and if they could invite family members to the event, that would be a great improvement.

There were a few obstacles to the planning of the summer event if the party was based on the survey results. First, their present budget did not include enough money to invite family members. Second, in order to offer the types of shared activities people wanted, they would have to choose a place to have the event that was bigger than any of their previous party venues. And third, a new caterer would have to be found who was willing to provide both vegetarian and non-vegetarian fare.

The committee split up their duties and decided to meet again in two weeks to share what each had accomplished. The staff assistant from library HR and the reference librarian had presented their case for more money to the HR director, who in turn took the request to the library director. And as they had been so convincing, money was added to their budget. The two paraprofessionals – both whom had worked at the university for a long time – used their contacts to find out if the lawn in front of the library could possibly be used for their event. It was available, as long as classes were not in session on the day of the event. The branch librarian and one of the paraprofessionals from the circulation desk created a list of possible caterers, divided the list in half, and each called all the businesses on their list. They each asked the caterers to send them menus and pricing information, as well enquiring about the vegetarian possibilities.

Two weeks later, when they met as a group for their next meeting, they quickly got the information sharing out of the way. And as they had all achieved their tasks, they got down to the actual party planning.

A month later, after much advertising, planning, organising, soliciting help from other staff members, and all the other things that go into throwing a party, the big day arrived. The caterer had brought plenty of food, and no one was disappointed (neither vegetarians nor carnivores). The dunking booth, volleyball, and three legged races between departments were a complete success. And all the spouses and kids who showed up had a terrific time.

At the debriefing meeting, every member of the group reported that they had not heard any complaints. The library party had been a complete success.

Questions

1. What made the party planning for this event different from how they had done it in the past?

2. How do you suppose future groups will benefit from how this group did its work?

Further reading

Agomah, A. (2005) 'Around the world, and back to Nigeria: the information technology (IT) centre at Rivers State University of Science and Technology, Port Harcourt, Nigeria'. *Library Hi Tech News* 22(7): 15–19.

Allee, N. and Savage D. C. (1998) 'Critical engagement: the merging of public health information resources'. *Library Hi Tech* 16(1): 84–90.

Allen, M., Ward, S. M. and Wray, T. (2003) 'Patron-focused services in three US libraries: collaborative interlibrary loan, collection development and acquisitions'. *Interlending & Document Supply* 31(2): 138–41.

Backhus, S. H. and Summey, T. P. (2003) 'Collaboration: the key to unlocking the dilemma of distance reference services'. *The Reference Librarian* (83/84): 193–202.

Bandelin, J. M. and Payne, J. K. (2000) 'Collaboration and reallocation: implementing a new collection development model at Furman University'. *Against the Grain* 12(5): 40–5.

Chao, S.-Y. J. (2001) 'Library cooperation on overseas chinese studies: from resource sharing to the development of library collections'. *Collection Building* 20(3): 123–30.

Chrisfield, T., Cosgrove, R. and Stinson, J. (2000) 'Building scholarly online multimedia collections and services'. *The Electronic Library* 18(5): 328–36.

Cooper, J. L. (2000) 'A model for library support of distance education in the USA'. *Interlending & Document Supply* 28(3): 123–31.

Cronin, C., Lage, K. and Long H. (2005) 'The flight plan of a digital initiatives project: providing remote access to aerial photographs of colorado'. *OCLC Systems & Services* 21(2): 114–30.

Dickinson, J. B., George, S. E. and Blackwell, L. S. (2005) 'Using collaboration to counteract inertia in a small library'. *The Serials Librarian* 48(5): 251–6.

Dugdale, C. (1999) 'Managing electronic reserves: new opportunities and new roles for academic librarians?' *Librarian Career Development* 7(12): 150–63.

Engle, M. (1998) 'The social position of electronic text centers'. *Library Hi Tech* 16(3/4): 15–20.

Guthrie, K. M. (1998) 'JSTOR and the University of Michigan: an evolving collaboration'. *Library Hi Tech* 16(1): 9–14.

Heenan, V. S. (2000) 'Electronic reserves: an opportunity for collaboration at William Paterson University'. *Journal of Interlibrary Loan, Document Delivery & Information Supply* 11(1): 29–37.

Hilliger, K. and Roberts, S. (2001) 'Key skills through collaboration: a library and information services and business, management and leisure partnership'. *Vine* 31(1): 10–16.

Holmes, G. V. and Howson, C. K. (2000) 'Grants: interdepartmental collaboration to teach grantsmanship skills'. *The Bottom Line: Managing Library Finances* 13(3): 146–50.

Jantz, R. and Bell, R. (2002) 'English advice manuals online at Rutgers: a partnership in a new course using digital books and web technology'. *Library Hi Tech* 20(3): 318–24.

Kemp, J. H. and Dillon, D. J. (1989) 'Collaboration and the accuracy imperative: improving reference service now. Librarians at the Perry-Castaneda Library, University of Texas at Austin, in June 1988 for a Half-Day Retreat'. *Reference Quarterly* 29: 62–70.

Lenholt, R., Costello, B. and Stryker, J. (2003) 'Utilizing Blackboard to provide library instruction: uploading MS Word handouts with links to course specific resources'. *Reference Services Review* 31(3): 211–18.

Mackay, M. (2001) 'Collaboration and liaison: the importance of developing working partnerships in the provision of networked hybrid services to lifelong learners in rural areas'. *Library Management* 22(8/9): 411–16.

Neal, J. G. (1997) 'College sports and library fundraising'. *The Bottom Line: Managing Library Finances* 10(2): 58–9.

Nitecki, D. A. and Rando W. (2004) 'A library and teaching center collaboration to assess the impact of using digital images on teaching, learning, and library support'. *Vine* 34(3): 119–25.

Rockman, I. F. (2002) 'Establishing successful partnerships with university support units'. *Library Management* 23(4/5): 192–8.

Snyder, C. A., Carter, H. and Soltys, M. (2002) 'ATC: all that collaboration at Southern Illinois University-Carbondale'. *Library Administration & Management* 16(4): 194–7.

Stoffel, B. and Cunningham, J. (2005) 'Library participation in campus web portals: an initial survey'. *Reference Services Review* 33(2): 144–60.

Taylor, L. R. and Taylor, M. (2004) 'Talking tech: communicating and collaborating more effectively with your IT support staff'. *Library Hi Tech News* 21(2): 25–6.

Ward, S. M., Wray, T. and Debus-Lopez, K. E. (2003) 'Collection development based on patron requests: collaboration between interlibrary loan and acquisitions'. *Library Collections, Acquisitions, and Technical Services* 27(2): 203–13.

Wessling, J. and Delaney, T. (2003) 'Rapid: a new level of collaboration for Ill'. *Colorado Libraries* 29(1): 22–4.

9

External collaboration

Overview

The cases in this chapter focus on external collaboration. These types of collaborations can take place at any level of the library hierarchy, but often happen higher up the organisation chart. They might involve budgetary issues or broad issues facing libraries, such as preservation, disaster plans, or scholarly communication. They often include the involvement of librarians who must collaborate beyond their own library because they have no subject or work responsibility peer at their own institution. For example, it is highly unlikely that a library system will have more than one East Asian subject librarian. External collaborations – often begun because of an obvious or pressing shared need or frequently just a shared interest – need the close cooperative work of many participants from a wide variety of libraries and institutions for them to succeed.

Challenges to external collaborations can include overcoming differences in budgets and bureaucracies of different institutions, geographical separation – both near and far, time differences, and as in the previous chapters, differences in work styles, work schedules, ethics, long-term schedules, subject disciplines and work loads.

These case studies examining external collaboration – described below and listed in our reference section – cover a gamut of collaboration types and as with those discussed in Chapter 7, are really only limited by your imagination and willingness to take risks and be flexible. Because there are vast differences between institutions and the work of the librarians, faculty and staff who work at them, these types of collaborations can be very challenging, yet are often the most rewarding types of collaborations for all participants, and can be the collaborations that last the longest and morph into many other types of collaborative projects.

External collaborations are often the hardest types of collaborations, as the opportunities for things to go wrong are multiplied by the number of challenges. As we mention in Chapters 6 and 7, with any collaboration if you find them turning sour, turn back to the first section of this book and try using some of the tools and tips to see if you can improve your collaboration the next time around. Don't give up! We have found that many collaborations can start out slow, or on the wrong foot, but can be brought back on track with some re-adjustments.

Plagiarism tutorial case study

- *Participants*: instruction and subject librarians, library school interns, undergraduate students along with the assistance from faculty, instructional technology specialists, and library web services.
- *Institutions/departments/others involved*: private university.
- *Type of collaboration*: creating an online tutorial.
- *Length of collaboration*: six months of development for the first version, 12 months of testing and revising for the release of the final version.

- *Advantages*: leveraging the expertise and insight from a wide array of participants and groups.

- *Outcomes*: an online plagiarism tutorial made accessible to the university community.

Case narrative

A survey on academic dishonesty administered to a sampling of students and faculty at private university in 2000 revealed some surprising results. Nearly half of the students admitted to having collaborated with other students on their work without faculty permission. Nearly 40 per cent of the students admitted to having copied a few sentences in their papers without footnoting them in the bibliography. Only around a third of the students thought that falsifying a bibliography constituted serious cheating, while only a quarter of the students felt that unauthorised collaboration was wrong. Two-thirds of the faculty surveyed thought students had a low or very low understanding of the university's policy on student cheating while even more respondents thought that the faculty's own understanding of the policy was inadequate.

In an effort to counter the students' lackadaisical attitude towards academic dishonesty, the university's Council for Academic Integrity approached the library about developing an online plagiarism tutorial. The library assembled a team to work on the project that consisted of instruction and subject librarians, library school interns from a local state university, and undergraduate students. The team's first task was determining the target audience. The main group they wanted to reach was undergraduates who are vulnerable to plagiarism. To make sure they were targeting this audience, the group wanted the tutorial's content to be based on the university's own definition of plagiarism. This would prevent the tutorial from having a generic feel. The group also wanted to attract faculty to the site with a collection of resources geared towards instructors, but they were uncertain if faculty would use the tutorial.

The team's early discussion also concerned picking a platform on which to make the tutorial accessible. They decided that the final version would eventually have its own standalone website. Because web development takes time, however, and because the team wanted to make the tutorial rapidly available for beta testing, the first version of the tutorial would be posted on Blackboard, the course management software. Blackboard would allow for easy posting of the content, it is accessible to all students and faculty at the university, and it allows the team to easily gather feedback on the tutorial.

With some key decisions on audience and technology made, the group came up with a timeline for developing the tutorial. The group used Microsoft Project, a project management program, to develop the timeline. The first phase, which lasted four months, consisted of fleshing out ideas on the content, technology, and marketing of the tutorial. The group collaborated closely with the university's Council for Academic Integrity, trying to incorporate the ideas and suggestions from the Council into the early planning. The group also used this time to study other online plagiarism tutorials to determine what was effective and what wasn't.

The second phase, which lasted two months, involved creating the content for the tutorial. Much of the group's work was guided by the earlier meeting with the Council for Academic Integrity. Group members were divided up into groups and each group was assigned different sections of the tutorial to work on. One section consisted of addressing the situations that might cause students to plagiarise or cheat (e.g. being overwhelmed by schoolwork, being uncertain of how to cite). It was useful that the undergraduates on the team were helping to write this section because they could provide real-life insight into this matter. Members of the group shared work over e-mail so others in the group would have a chance to edit and comment on it. The team also had regular meetings during this phase to make sure everyone was on track and to allow for face-to-face collaboration. Scheduling these meetings was a challenge because there were around ten group members collaborating on the content, and they didn't all work at the same location.

Phase three, which lasted a month, consisted of mounting the content onto Blackboard. Transferring the content to the course management software offered some challenges because Blackboard's navigation is less flexible than that of a regular website. To provide greater usability of the Blackboard site, the group collaborated with the university's Center for Classroom Technology (CCT). CCT offers consulting to the university community on applying technology in the classroom, and they have worked with numerous faculty and researchers on instructional projects. As CCT administers Blackboard for the university, the team used their expertise and got advice and support on mounting the site and creating a more user-friendly interface.

Once the tutorial was available on the Blackboard site, it underwent beta testing for four weeks as part of phase four. The team encouraged stakeholders (students, faculty, teaching assistants, librarians) to comment on the content and layout of the tutorials. These comments were used by the group to revise the tutorial for its Blackboard release. The revised tutorial was made available to all faculty to be used by students in their classes. The testing and revising of the tutorial continued and tutorial users were encouraged to send in comments to the group. Members of the group also demonstrated the tutorial to relevant organisations on campus, such as the Student Government Association, in order to get additional feedback. The group collected and documented this feedback so it could be incorporated in the web version of the tutorial.

The group collaborated with CCT once again to seek guidance on transferring the tutorial from Blackboard to the Web. Based on advice from CCT and from feedback from the numerous stakeholders, the tutorial was mounted on the Web by the library's web services department. The standalone web version offers easier navigation of the tutorial's content, and the site is also accessible to those users who aren't logged into Blackboard. Although the standalone web version of the tutorial is the final end product of the group, revisions will continue to the site based on feedback from users.

Questions

1. Why did the collaborators decide to include so many partners?

2. What planning and evaluation techniques did they use?

3. What are some next steps for this project?

White paper

- *Participants*: subject librarians, reference librarians, consortium programme director.

- *Institutions/departments/others involved*: consortium, private university, three state universities.

- *Type of collaboration*: writing a white paper for a consortial project.

- *Length of collaboration*: six months of development for the first version, 12 months of testing, revising and release of the final version.

- *Advantages*: leveraging the expertise and insight from a specific group of librarians with similar subject backgrounds.

- *Outcomes*: a white paper on storing shared last copies of science, technology and medial serials within the consortia.

Case narrative

The science, technology and medicine (STM) collections working group had reached the last item on the agenda of their biannual meeting. As this was added to the agenda by the consortium project director, she started by describing the paper the executive committee of the consortium would like the working group to research and write. As all the consortium member libraries were rapidly running out of space, particularly space for collections, and the cost for storing library materials was high, the director wanted the STM group to prepare a white paper on what would be the implications, payoff, and basic logistics of storing and then sharing within the consortium, a single copy of every STM serial back file placed in storage. The project director offered to be a part of a smaller working group and also gave them the deadline for the paper set by the executive committee of the consortium.

The chairperson of the STM group suggested that they have a general discussion of the topic, and then she would ask for volunteers to work on the paper with herself and the project director. She also said that she would like to keep the group small and wanted to make sure it was representative of all the subject areas. After the discussion, four librarians from the group raised their hands to volunteer, and the chairperson took down their names and said they would be hearing from her.

A few days later the chairperson sent an e-mail to all those who expressed interest as well as the project director. She welcomed them to the group, thanked them for volunteering, asked them to check their calendars against the schedule presented later in the e-mail, and then gave them a list of items to start thinking about before they came to the first meeting. All of the group members had answered within one day, so the meeting was set, and the project director offered to have the group meet in the consortium's meeting room located at one of the state universities.

The chairperson wanted to make sure that the project did not take up too much time of any of the members, especially face-to-face time. She also knew that though the consortial member libraries were all within 30 minutes drive of one another, for all of the working group members to have to leave campus for multiple meetings, as well as the nightmare of scheduling the meetings so that all of the participants could attend, would be a major obstacle to getting the white paper written. So, knowing this, she concluded that with one initial meeting, where they planned out the project, divided up the work, and set deadlines for draft completion, the group could conduct all the rest of its work using e-mail. Perhaps the chairperson and the project director could get together to hash out the final draft for presentation to the executive committee, but it would work best of the full group only had to meet face-to-face once.

The chairperson then e-mailed the working group describing her plan. She then told them that agreeing to this plan would mean that they would all have to be prepared to jump right in and start working at the first and only meeting. To get them prepared for that meeting, she asked each of them to find at least one article germane to the topic and read it before they came to the meeting. She also asked them to take some time to think about what the different sections of the white paper should be, and what parts they would be most likely to write.

At the meeting, one of the first acts of business was thanking the project director for hosting the meeting as well as providing all of them with parking passes. Then the group, as requested ahead of time, got right to work. They quickly mapped out the different sections of the white paper, and all volunteered to write more than one part. Knowing ahead of time that they would only be required to come to one meeting ensured that each of them would stay focused on what they needed to do.

Next they created a schedule. After it was mostly complete, half of the members really wanted to include some time to send out first drafts of their sections by e-mail. So they rearranged what they had already done to build in time for sharing of the first draft. They all left the meeting knowing exactly what they were responsible for and when they had to complete it by. The chairperson walked back to her car happy that everyone had been very engaged and productive in the meeting.

The deadlines came and every person sent in their first, and then their final drafts out to the entire group. Each member shared comments and ideas on the drafts to the authors. And for the assembly of the final copy, the chairperson and the project director set up a time to meet and put it together.

Once the white paper was complete, the final version was sent by e-mail to all of the working group members for one last look over. Once all the members had replied that it was ready to go, the project director brought it to the next meeting of the consortium's executive committee. The chairperson sent handwritten thank-you notes to all of the members of the working group, telling each of them how much she appreciated their willingness to work within the confines of the project structure and congratulated them on their hard work and excellent writing.

Questions

1. What other ways could the working group have used to accomodate their scheduling and geographic challenges?

2. Do you think the members will volunteer for another project group chaired by the same person?

3. Why? Or why not?

Further reading

Allard, S. (2002) 'Digital libraries and organizations for international collaboration and knowledge creation'. *The Electronic Library* 20(5): 369–81.

Allen, D. and Wilson, T. D. (1995) 'The context of information strategies: competition or collaboration?' *New Review of Academic Librarianship* 1: 3–14.

Arnold, K. and Ramsden, A. (1995) 'The electronic library: an opportunity for collaboration? A case study based on the Elinor Project at De Montfort (I.E. Montfort) University Milton Keynes. Presented at the IATUL Seminar, Sheffield, England, July 1994'. *IATUL Proceedings new ser* 4: 186–93.

Ashworth, S. and Joint, N. (2003) 'A model for inter-institutional collaboration: the Gaels Project document delivery trials'. *Library Review* 52(4): 150–8.

Bailey-Hainer, B. and Urban, R. (2004) 'The Colorado Digitization Program: a collaboration success story'. *Library Hi Tech* 22(3): 254–62.

Benner, M. (2003) 'The digital archive of the Swedish East India Company, 1731–1813: A joint project of a university library and a history department'. *Online Information Review* 27(5): 328–32.

Bradley, D. R., Kelly, J. A. and Wilhelm, C. (1998) 'Healthweb: an internet collaboration among librarians at universities in the CIC'. *College & Research Libraries News* 59(5): 338–40.

Brenneise, H. R. and Marks, E. B. (2001) 'Creating a state-wide virtual health library: The Michigan experience'. *Online Information Review* 25(2): 115–20.

Brisson, R. (2000) 'The German Resources Project: the promise of technology in fostering international collaboration'. *Library Hi Tech* 18(3): 234–55.

Burroughs, C. M. (2004) 'Evaluation in health information outreach programs'. *Reference Services Review* 32(1): 64–8.

Carpenter, K. H. (1996) 'Competition, collaboration, and cost in the new knowledge environment'. *Collection Management* 21(2): 31–46.

Chao, S.-Y. J. (2001) 'A model of library cooperation on overseas Chinese studies: the Ohio experience'. *Collection Building* 20(2): 45–53.

Clareson, T. F. R. (1990) 'Education, communication, and cooperation: OCLC'S preservation program'. *OCLC Systems & Services* 6(6): 10–12.

Cole, T. W. and Shreeves, S. L. (2004) 'The IMLS NLG program: fostering collaboration'. *Library Hi Tech* 22(3): 246–48.

Comer, C. H. and Ricker, A. S. (2002) 'New roles and global collaboration. International conference hosted by Yunnan University, Kunming, China'. *College & Research Libraries News* 63(2): 106–8.

Cox, J. (2000) 'Developing model licenses for electronic resources: cooperation in a competitive world'. *Library Consortium Management: An International Journal* 2(1): 8–17.

Cox, R. and Onuf, R. (2003) 'Digital anxiety and cooperation in a networked world'. *OCLC Systems & Services* 19(1): 36–40.

Cramond, S. (1999) 'Efforts to formalise international collaboration in scholarly information infrastructure'. *Library Hi Tech* 17(3): 272–82.

Daniels, B. E. (1996) 'State libraries: architects for the information highway'. *Internet Research* 6(4): 33–6.

Diller, K. R. (1997) 'Helping your campus navigate electronic environments: collaboration is a necessity. Instructional program administered and taught by members of the Library and the Information Technology Department at Washington State University, Vancouver'. *Research Strategies* 15(3): 187–92.

Donovan, M. H. (1992) 'Fifth Japan-US conference on libraries and information science in higher education (6–9 October 1992, Tokyo): Japan–US collaboration in enhancing international access to scholarly information; looking toward the 21st century'. *Committee on East Asian Libraries Bulletin* 97: 21–2.

Downer, S., Medina, S. and Nicol B. (2005) 'Alabamamosaic: sharing Alabama history online'. *Library Hi Tech* 23(2): 233–51.

Elkington, N. E. and Massie, D. (1999) 'The changing nature of international resource sharing: risks and benefits of collaboration'. *Interlending & Document Supply* 27(4): 148–54.

Evans, G. E. (2002) 'Management issues of consortia: part two'. *Library Management* 23(6/7): 275–86.

Fabbi, J. L., Watson, S. D., Marks, K. E. and Sylvis, Z. (2005) 'UNLV libraries and the digital identification frontier'. *Library Hi Tech* 23(3): 313–22.

Farmer, L. S. J. (2003) 'Facilitating faculty incorporation of information literacy skills into the curriculum through the use of online instruction'. *Reference Services Review* 31(4): 307–12.

Fifarek, A. (2002) 'Celebrating history and innovation: The Louisiana Purchase Digital Library Project at Louisiana State University'. *OCLC Systems & Services* 18(4): 186–94.

Fisher, M. (2003) 'Biomedical journal collaboration in London: development of the union database'. *Program: Electronic Library And Information Systems* 37(4): 234–41.

Friend, F. J. (2002) 'Improving access: is there any hope?' *Interlending & Document Supply* 30(4): 183–9.

Gammon, J. A. and Zeoli, M. (2003) 'The Ohiolink-YBP road shows: a partnership for vendor/library collaboration'. *Library Collections, Acquisitions, and Technical Services* 27(2): 139–45.

Guthrie, K. M. (1998) 'JSTOR and the University of Michigan: an evolving collaboration'. *Library Hi Tech* 16(1): 9–14.

Haak, J., Josephine, H. B. and Miyataki, G. (1995) 'Information services and economic development: new opportunities for collaboration. Fee-based library external services program at the University of Hawaii at Manoa'. *Journal of Library Administration* 20(3–4): 57–79.

Hartman, C. N., Beldon, D., Reis, N. K., Alemneh, D.G., Phillips, M. and Dunlop, D. (2005) 'Development of a portal to Texas history'. *Library Hi Tech* 23(2): 151–63.

Hedegaard, R. (2004) 'The benefits of archives, libraries and museums working together: a Danish case of shared databases'. *New Library World* 105(7/8): 290–6.

Heery, R. (2000) 'Information gateways: collaboration on content'. *Online Information Review* 24(1): 40–5.

Hodges, D. and Lunau, C. D. (1999) 'The national library of Canada's digital library initiatives'. *Library Hi Tech* 17(2): 152–64.

Hope, C. B. and Peterson, C. A. (2002) 'The sum is greater than the parts: cross-institutional collaboration for information literacy in academic libraries'. *Journal of Library Administration* 36(1/2): 21–38.

Hughes, C. A. (2004) 'Escholarship at the University of California: a case study in sustainable innovation for open access'. *New Library World* 105(3/4): 118–24.

Huxley, L. (2001) 'Renardus: fostering collaboration between academic subject gateways in Europe'. *Online Information Review* 25(2): 121–7.

Huxley, L., Carpenter, L. and Peereboom, M. (2003) 'The Renardus broker service: collaborative frameworks and tools'. *The Electronic Library* 21(1): 39–48.

Jakubs, D. (2000) 'The AAU/ARL global resources program: origins and trajectory'. *Library Hi Tech* 18(3): 209–14.

Jalloh, B. (1999) 'A plan for the establishment of a library network or consortium for Swaziland: preliminary investigations and formulations'. *Interlending & Document Supply* 27(4): 158–65.

Jesudason, M. (1993) 'Academic libraries and outreach services through precollege programs: a proactive collaboration. Experience of the University of Wisconsin, Madison'. *Reference Services Review* 21(4): 29–36.

Johnson, C. P., Brodeen, G. and Humeston, H. (2001) 'Collaboration generates synergy: Saint Paul Public Library, the College of St. Catherine, and the 'Family Place' program'. *Reference & User Services Quarterly* 41(1): 19–23.

Joiner, C., Lewis, L. K. and Mackler, T. (1993) 'Albuquerque alliance: library/bookstore collaboration for collection building; Tasha's paperback books helps the University of New Mexico Library collect novels by state authors and/or those set in the state'. *Library Journal* 118: 75–6.

Kayler, G. and Pival, P. R. (2004) 'Working together: effective collaboration in a consortium environment'. *Journal of Library Administration* 41(1/2): 203–15.

Lammay, B. W. (1996) 'Collaboration helps achieve student success for Henrico County Public Schools'. *Virginia Libraries* 42: 11–12.

Lavagnino, M. B. (1999) 'Authentication, bandwidth, and collaboration: the library systems directors' ABCs'. *Library Hi Tech* 17(4): 396–402.

Lippincott, J. K. (2004) 'New library facilities: opportunities for collaboration'. *Resource Sharing and Information Networks* 17(1/2): 147–57.

Lougee, W. P. (1998) 'The University of Michigan digital library program: a retrospective on collaboration within the academy'. *Library Hi Tech* 16(1): 51–9.

Mackay, M. (2001) 'Collaboration and liaison: the importance of developing working partnerships in the provision of networked hybrid services to lifelong learners in rural areas at the University of the Highlands and Islands'. *Library Management* 22(8/9): 411–15.

Matthews, G. and Thebridge, S. (2001) 'Preservation management training and education: developing a sector-wide approach'. *New Library World* 102(11/12): 443–52.

Maurer, M. B. and Hurst, M. L. (2003) 'Library-vendor collaboration for re-engineering workflow: The Kent State experience'. *Library Collections, Acquisitions, and Technical Services* 27(2): 155–64.

May, H. L. and Kocour, B. G. (2002) 'The Alice Library Instruction Toolbox: an exercise in collaboration. Appalachian library inter campus extension'. *Virginia Libraries* 48(3): 13–17.

McCrae, G., Hardinge, J. and Scrimgeour, D. (1992). 'Interactive on-line acquisitions using BEDIS: three perspectives'. *New Library World* 93(1): 15–17.

McDonald, J. and Bolland, K. (2003) 'Collaboration and resource sharing in and from the south pacific: The National Library of New Zealand'. *Interlending & Document Supply* 31(2): 117–22.

Melrose, E. A. (2004) 'The North Yorkshire Unnetie Digitisation Project: from an idea to an opportunity'. *New Library World* 105(5/6): 196–202.

Milne, R. R. (2002) 'The "Distributed National Collection" access and cross-sectoral collaboration: The Research Support Libraries Programme'. *Ariadne (Online).* 31 March/April: Libraries Worldwide: 89.

Mirsky, P. S. (2003) 'The University of California's collection development collaboration: a campus perspective'. *Collection Management* 28(1/2): 55–61.

Mittler, E. (1989) 'Academic research libraries in Germany: The Heidelberg experience; a century of collaboration based on a talk at the Fifth ACRL National Conference in Cincinnati, April 7, 1989'. *College & Research Libraries News* 9: 826–8.

Nahl, D., Coder, A. and Black, J. (1994) 'Effectiveness of fieldwork at an information desk: a prototype for academic library-library school collaboration at the University of Hawaii'. *The Journal of Academic Librarianship* 20: 291–4.

Nickerson, M. F. (2004) 'Online multimedia museum exhibits: a case study in technology and collaboration'. *Library Hi Tech* 22(3): 270–76.

Nye, J. and Magier, D. (2000) 'International information exchange: new configurations for library collaboration in South Asian Studies. Presented at the CRL conference,

November 1999, Atlanta, Georgia'. *Collection Management* 24(3/4): 215–39.

O'Connor, S. (2002) 'Research is the basis of a collaborative solution for academic libraries: The Victorian Academic Digital Library (VADL)'. *Library Management* 23(8/9): 417–21.

Peereboom, M. (2000) 'Dutchess: Dutch Electronic Subject Service – a Dutch national collaborative effort'. *Online Information Review* 24(1): 46–9.

Peyton, G. and Bonfanti, P. G. (2005) 'Library campus outreach collaboration at Mississippi State University'. *Mississippi Libraries* 69(1): 11–12.

Pharo, S. (2004) 'Crossroads, traffic-lights or roundabouts? Collaboration now and in the future of New Zealand's tertiary education libraries'. *Library Management* 25(3): 98–103.

Pival, P. R. and Johnson, K. (2004) 'Tri-institutional library support: a lesson in forced collaboration'. *Journal of Library Administration* 41(3/4): 345–54.

Premkamolnetr, N. (2004) 'Collaboration between a technological university library and tenant firms in a technology park in Thailand: new challenges for librarianship in a developing country'. *Asian Libraries* 8: 224–38.

Reed, C. (1991) 'OCLC: the original idea'. *OCLC Systems & Services* 7(2): 6–8.

Riggs, C. (2004) 'Coalition of networked information (CNI) task force meeting'. *Library Hi Tech News* 21(6): 3–4.

Roper, F. W., Barron, D. D. and Funk C. J. (1996) 'Collaboration in a continuum of learning: developing the next generation of leadership. Partnership of MLA, the University of South Carolina and LISDEC'. *Bulletin of the Medical Library Association* 84: 549–52.

Rudge, S. and Wilson, I. (2001) 'Electronic information delivery: joint working at UCE'. *Vine* 31(1): 41–7.

Sandelands, E. (1998) 'Creating an online library to support a virtual learning community'. *Internet Research* 8(1): 75–80.

Sanz, P. (2005) 'Distributed collections and central repository in France: competition or complementarity?' *Library Management* 26(1/2): 49–56.

Scepanski, J. M. and Von Wahlde, B. A. (1998) 'Megasystem collaboration: cross-continent consortial cooperation. Revision of paper presented at the 1996 Crimea International Conference'. *Information Technology and Libraries* 17(1): 30–5.

Schlesinger, J. B. (1999) 'Meeting the instructional technology challenge: institutional collaboration and faculty development. Lehigh Valley Hospital and Medical College of Virginia'. *Medical Reference Services Quarterly* 18(2): 91–6.

Sharma, R. N. and Bess, J. (2000) 'West Virginia to West Africa and back: an intercontinental collaboration between West Virginia State College and the National University of Benin'. *American Libraries* 31(7): 44–6.

Shepherd, M. (1999) 'The truth is in the details: lessons from library collaboration'. *Library Management* 20(33): 2–7.

Shim, W. and McClure, C. R. (2002) 'Improving database vendors usage statistics reporting through collaboration between libraries and vendors'. *College & Research Libraries* 63(6): 499–514.

Shin, E.-J. and Oh, K.-M. (2002) 'Interlending and document supply developments in South Korea'. *Interlending & Document Supply* 30(3): 136–38.

Simpson, D. B. (1997) 'Solving the challenges presented by electronic resources: creating opportunities through inter-institutional collaboration. Center for Research Libraries; Presented at the 1997 University of Oklahoma Conference'. *Journal of Library Administration* 24(4): 49–60.

Smethurst, M. (1991) 'The British Library and university libraries: a personal reflection upon cooperation between libraries serving scholarship and research'. *Library Review* 40(2): 96–108.

Stäglich, D. (1985) 'Die Zusammenarbeit mit den Personalräten bei der Einführung der EDV in den Hochschulbibliotheken Nordrhein-Westfalens'. *Zeitschrift für Bibliothekswesen und Bibliographie* 32: 389–400.

Sugarman, T. S. and Demetracopoulos, C. (2001) 'Creating a web research guide: collaboration between liaisons, faculty and students at Georgia State University'. *Reference Services Review* 29(2): 150–6.

Truelson, J. A. (2004) 'Partnering on virtual reference using Questionpoint: Guidelines for collaboration between academic libraries in Australia/New Zealand and the US'. *Australian Academic & Research Libraries* 35(4): 301–8.

Vinopal, J. (2002) 'The humanities computing center and library collaboration in new scholarly communication processes'. *Advances in Librarianship* V26. Burlington, MA: Academic Press; pp. 91–126.

Walker, J. (2001) 'Open linking for libraries: the Openurl framework'. *New Library World* 102(4/5): 127–34.

Ward, R. (2003) 'NMAP: The UK's nursing internet gateway'. *Vine* 33(2): 78–82.

Warren, G. (2002) 'The English experience – library and information services, delivering access collaboratively'. *Interlending & Document Supply* 30(4): 195–202.

West, R. P. (1998) 'The need for collaboration to build the knowledge infrastructure. Presented at the Conference Challenging Marketplace Solutions to Problems in the Economics of Information, September 1995, Washington, DC'. *Journal of Library Administration* 26(1–2): 251–9.

Wicks, D. A., Bartolo, L. M. and Swords, D. A. (2001) 'Four birds with one stone: collaboration in collection development at Kent State University'. *Library Collections, Acquisitions, and Technical Services* 25(4): 473–83.

Wilson, L. A. (2000) 'The lone ranger is dead: success today demands collaboration'. *College & Research Libraries News* 61(8): 698–701.

Wykoff, L., Mercier, L., Bond, T. and Cornish, A. (2005) 'The Columbia River Basin Ethnic History Archive: a tri-state online history database and learning center'. *Library Hi Tech* 23(2): 252–64.

Yao, X., Chen, L. and Dai, L. (2004) 'Current situation and future development of CALIS'. *Library Management* 25(6/7): 277–82.

Zappen, S. H. (1997) 'From cancellations to collaboration – some thoughts: handling rising serial costs at Skidmore College'. *Against the Grain* 9: 1.

Index